EVERY SINGLE DAY

DAILY HABITS TO CREATE UNSTOPPABLE
SUCCESS, ACHIEVE GOALS FASTER, AND
UNLEASH YOUR EXTRAORDINARY POTENTIAL

BRADLEY CHARBONNEAU

REPOSSIBLE

For my Dad

PRAISE FOR EVERY SINGLE DAY

"Bradley is an inspiration and a leader. He reminds each of us that **we too can become consistent and unstoppable.**"

— DEANNE WELSH

"**Deliciousness to my soul**, is the description that comes to mind as I reflect on my experience of consuming this book. I have no idea how to write a review and put into words **how deeply this resonated within me.**

There's a spark within me that has been relit. I know **ESD is the kindling I need to get the fire crackling and roaring** ... there are flames here that need to breathe and light the world.

Thank you Bradley Charbonneau for accepting the challenge of ESD, so that today, you could influence my ESD."

— 5 STARS FROM P.C.

"Before reading this book I was ashamed of myself.

For years I had called myself an artist but I knew the truth. I was only masquerading as one. ... But could I continue to call myself an artist when I stoped making artwork? The answers is no.

I **developed a fear** of making artwork. I would always make excuses as to why I just couldn't create. I was too tired, the dog needed a bath, I needed to do dishes. What was the point of painting anyway **because no one would want to buy or look at my work** etc.

After reading this book, there is no going back. I have no choice.

I make artwork everyday and **I am happy.** ... I know there is no going back.

I was miserable with guilt and now I am not.

I was afraid to create and now I happy to learn once more.

I wrote this review in the hope that I could inspire someone else to change their life.

Take the Every Single Day challenge. Read this book it just might change your life."

— Paige

"The author shows us how to get past "**analysis paralysis**" to actually start projects and see them through until completion.

A theme of this book is to **dream about doing something until the dream itself is internalized along with the willingness to progress toward goal completion in iterative steps taken each day.**"

— Dr. Joseph S. Maresca, Amazon "Hall of Fame" Reviewer

"This author has provided an excellent "how to" book, to **move past procrastination**, and **getting past fear.**"

— ROBERT ENZENAUER

" ... for anyone with **dreams hidden in the attic, cellar or heart.**"

— AMAZON REVIEWER

"If you're ready to **live your dream** (as compared with simply dreaming your dream), **this book will help you do it.**"

— LAURIE KING

I work with people who cannot see past their current situation. Yet, they want to become more than who they are today. **This book is a tool I will use to help reach my clients.**

— TRACY GANNAWAY, PHYSICAL THERAPIST

"He lights a path that you can choose to walk down."

— RAY SIMON, ACCOMPLISHED SPEAKER, AND A NO-LONGER-SECRET TRUMPET PLAYER

" ... the result is **daily improvement** (even if doesn't feel that way when you're in the middle of it all)."

— RICHARD ROBINSON

"Found the benefits not limited to the idea of developing a habit and improving whatever it is you've chosen to do 'every single day' – The fact that you are achieving it does **wonders for your sense of self worth.**"

— SIMON VANCE

CONTENTS

Foreword   xiii
Introduction   xix
Preface   xxi

PART I
PRECAUTION

1. Introduction   3
2. The Devil at the Dinner Party   7
3. The Pill   14
4. Day Zero   16
5. Who are you?   18
6. Failure   19
7. Possible, Impossible, Repossible   21
8. You, Me, and Four Others   25

PART II
PROCRASTINATION

9. Introduction   29
10. The Perfect Storm   33
11. Purgatory   36
12. You know those things you never seem to get done?   38
13. The Conundrum of Comfortable   40

PART III
PASSION

14. Introduction   47
15. How do you know if you're ready to make "The Leap"?   50
16. You do it even when you don't want to.   53
17. I motivated him to start. He was inspired to stay.   55
18. The only productivity tip you'll ever need.   57
19. What if you had one decision less to make Every   60
    Single Day?
20. You can run, but you can't hide.   63

PART IV

PERSEVERANCE

21. Introduction	67
22. If you could practice more, would you?	69
23. Today is a whole lot easier to see as yesterday than as tomorrow.	71
24. Because "Every other day plus weekends" is too complicated.	74
25. You'll never again say, "Oh well. Another day where I didn't get it done."	77
26. The "how" no longer matters.	80
27. Practice is Perfect	83
28. Learning is Cumulative	86
29. The $23,135 Recurring Passive Income Post	88
30. Oh baby, it's cold outside. (AKA: No one will notice if we don't do this.)	91

PART V

PATIENCE

31. Introduction	97
32. Meditation is a single letter away from Medication ... and Mediation.	100
33. This is how you live to be 103 years old.	104
34. What if you could free up your brain to put your creativity into turbo overdrive?	107

PART VI

PLAY

35. Introduction	113
36. Linear vs. Exponential	116
37. Better Together	120
38. Coast	123
39. The Cruise Ship & The Sailboat	125
40. Yes, you can force the Flow State.	128
41. Expect the Unexpected	131

PART VII

PERORATION

42. Introduction	135
43. ESD Side Effects	137
44. Reality Check and the "Overnight Success"	142

45. When you hear about how a person changed her life,   144
it changes your life.

46. Freedom   146

PART VIII
POSTSCRIPT

47. Where to Go from Here   151

Afterword   153
Acknowledgments   155
About the Author   157
Also by Bradley Charbonneau   159
Excerpt from "Ask"   162
The End   166

FOREWORD

Wow. I sort of can't believe I'm doing this. Sitting down to write the foreword of Bradley's book. I'm honored, truly, but I still sort of can't believe I'm doing this. Part of me can't believe there's a book at all. There wasn't going to be one, I was pretty sure of that.

And if you'd known Bradley back in 2012, like I did, you wouldn't believe it either. If you'd asked me back then, I'd say there probably wasn't going to be a real live book. Certainly not a sixth book. Not one like this.

I worked with Bradley. I knew he was a "former writer" (his words). I knew he was good at his work, but he didn't love it. He loved writing, but he didn't actually write all that much. He had given it a shot, being a "real" writer, being a professional. He'd written and published a book, a travel guide. I'd read his essays and stories in magazines. They were really good. But that was his "former life." That's how he put it.

He would joke about it, but I now know it must have pained him. "I'm a travel writer who doesn't travel or write," he'd chuckle and say.

I remember walking one day with Bradley through the streets of San Francisco. There's a moment that sticks out to me. It didn't seem all that important at the time, but it does now. It was 2012, a rare sunny day in the late summer. We were talking about work and life and the usual topics friends talk about. We passed a little corner market with a green awning at the top of a hill in a not-so-great neighborhood. We were standing on the corner of Eddy and Leavenworth, waiting to cross the street.

And that's when he told me.

It smelled terrible and I could barely hear him over the traffic. He said it sort of meekly, too. But that's when he *really* told me about his dream of being a writer.

He opened up about the path he'd started to go down years earlier. How he'd "given it a shot for 9 months." How he'd decided to "be practical instead." He had a young family to support, and being practical was probably the right choice. But the way he said it, I could tell it still hurt. He told me how much joy he felt when he was writing. About the secret book he kept in a drawer. His great American novel. All the ideas he had and wanted to share but never put down on paper.

He would light up every time he talked about writing. It was clear he had a passion for it. But it wasn't a dream he was actively working on. I knew what had happened because the same thing has happened to me before.

He'd let his dream rust. He'd left it sitting for too long, like an old car, and all the gears were rusted and fused together. Nothing was as shiny as it once was. It wasn't really going anywhere. He wasn't driving it, and every time he looked at it, he felt a little bit worse.

Sure, he'd reminisce about the good old times, but I don't know if he truly believed they would come again. At best, it seemed bittersweet. He had lived his dream for a while, but he talked about it as a part of his past.

We'd have similar conversations sometimes, and his dream would come back into focus. I'd try to encourage him to write more often, to publish on his blog or maybe start a new one, or just go with pen and paper. Whatever. It started to come up in conversation more often.

As summer turned to fall, it seemed like the rust on Bradley's dream was starting to break loose, at least in his mind. Then one foggy morning in late October 2012, three guys walked into a cafe in downtown San Francisco. (I really wish I had a funny punchline to follow that sentence.) We sipped our enormous chai lattes and talked shop about our businesses.

Bradley confessed his writing dream to our other friend at the cafe. He talked about his writing days, about magazine articles and publishing his first book a decade earlier, about that *other* book, the "real" one in the drawer that just needed to be dusted off. He lit up as he talked about writing, about how he'd like to do it more, get back into it and *be a writer again.*

Most people stop there. They reminisce and talk about what they'd "like" to do differently, but nothing really changes. But that's not what happened next. Instead, I witnessed a true genesis moment.

Bradley said something really simple, yet profound. "A writer is someone who writes." I think he mostly said it to himself--he was the one who needed to hear it after all. You could see his eyes light up a little bit as he put the pieces together in his head.

Side-note: I happen to run a project where I challenge people to take on one-month personal experiments. So, sitting in the bustling cafe, I asked him, "What if you took on a challenge and wrote something every day for a month?"

He was ready. Excited. He said he'd up the ante and do one better. He'd write *and publish* something *every single day* for one month.

The next day was November 1st. He wrote and published this on his blog:

"I suffer from the typical writer's block. I see a blank screen and want to run. I think of editing some old work and cringe. I've been wanting to write on a regular basis for, oh, a decade. Not ten days, not ten months, but ten years. When oh when will that day come where I learn to write on a regular basis?

So here we go, it's November 1, 2012. I'm hoping, I'm even smiling to myself (no, really) that I'll look back on this day with pride and say that was the day that it all began. Whew, exhilarating." – Bradley Charbonneau, November 1, 2012.

And, so it began.

I honestly don't know how to describe what happened next because it's hard for me to believe it; but it's one of the best things I've ever had the privilege to witness. Bradley completed his challenge and wrote and published something every day for a month.

I saw him start to change right away. He became more excited and energetic. He'd say things like, "I'm feeling like a writer again" and "writing is bringing me closer to my kids" and "I'm falling back in love with writing." He didn't stop when the month was over.

He kept going.

He wrote and published something every day for 100 days, then 200, then 300, then a year, then 500 days. Every time he hit a milestone, he made a choice to keep going. He wrote and published a book with his kids on the 10-year anniversary of publishing his first book. Then he did it again a year later. He hit a thousand days in a row of writing and publishing something every single day.

He no longer resembled the mopey dejected "former writer" I'd known. He became unstoppable. A machine. It wasn't just about the writing, either. It was a deeper transformation. He became much more confident and bold. He was inspiring and even intimidating in some ways. He wasn't the same person anymore. He took risks and wrote books and closed his business and moved his family halfway across the world. He's done so many things I couldn't imagine "2012 Bradley" doing. That *he* couldn't imagine actually doing. I barely recognize my old friend these days, and I'm glad.

He realized his dream, and became a professional writer. This book is only a small piece of the proof of that.

Bradley told me I could write whatever I wanted in this foreword. I'm allowed to tell stories of how depressed and defeated he used to be about his dream, about how we had the same conversations over and over and over again. I think I've done enough of that. I've done enough of that in my own life, and if you're reading this book, I'm guessing you can understand that "before" picture well enough without me droning on about it.

So, I want to say a few final things.

I want to say that I am very very proud of my friend. That fact may not matter to you, reader, but it should. Because if there's something you want to do, something inside you that calls to you, your unrealized potential that you're not taking action toward, then you're probably not proud about it. I know it probably hurts in some ways.

Maybe you've let your dreams rust. Maybe it feels like shit to even think about them. This book was written for you. I want you to know that it's possible to change. It is possible to do things you can't imagine right now. I want you to do what it takes to be proud of yourself. I want you to stop waiting for inspiration or motivation, because those things only come *after* you take action on something that matters to you.

Use this book as a guide. Hell, don't wait to get started until after you've read it. Start now. The title is all you really need to know, but there is great value beneath the surface. Those pills on the cover, they are the prescription you are looking for. But the true value isn't even about what you think it's about--there's a secret that reveals itself as you dig deeper. It's about the courage and pride you earn by being consistent with something that's hard at first. This is medicine you take for the side effects.

If there's something you really want to do or become, just start doing it.

You can create amazing art, exercise your body to become stronger and more fit, build a great business or relationship, or hone a skill to the point of mastery. You just have to start doing it. Do it *every single day* until it becomes a part of you that won't go away. It's really that simple. You just have to decide.

Make today the day you look back on with pride and say, "That was the day that it all began."

We are all rooting for you.

-- John Muldoon

September 2017, San Francisco, CA

INTRODUCTION

Dear Reader,

You are about to embark on a series of small steps that can lead to major changes in your life.

You can turn this page on your own but I would like to invite you to join the Every Single Day Community so we can travel this path together.

In the ESD Community, you will get:

1. Practical, actionable tips to change your daily habits
2. Early access to future books
3. Free or discounted codes to audiobooks
4. 10-Day Inspirational Challenges
5. Motivational videos
6. Recipes for change
7. Recipes for burritos
8. Early bird access to events (online and in person)

Sign up at esd.repossible.com.

PREFACE

Research has shown that it takes 31 days of conscious effort to make or break a habit. That means, if one practices something consistently for 31 days, on the 32nd day it does become a habit. Information has been internalised into behavioural change, which is called transformation.

— SHIV KHERA

"Transformation."

Woooo. Big word! Scary. Impressive. Unattainable.

I even used the word in one of my earlier subtitles, "A prescription for transformation." Sounds big and important. Probably takes forever and you might have to sacrifice a kidney to get it.

Let's start this book off with a light and simple version of transformation.

Transformation doesn't take as long as you might think and doesn't have to change your entire life.

In this book, you'll learn about patience and perseverance and how I spent 26 years slogging away avoiding living my dream. Ouch. Painful. Yuck. Heavy. Boring.

But the actual "transformation" part? Yeah, that probably took a few seconds.

I transformed myself when I made the decision to change my behavior.

It took more than two decades to ponder and wish, hope and delay, pretend, and defer. Then a few mere moments to crush it all with a simple decision to change a single daily behavior--and stick with that new behavior.

That about sums up this book.

I might threaten you with gargantuan monsters of topics in this book, but I'll usually give you binoculars with which, when you turn them around, you transform that beast into a sweet fuzzy chinchilla.

Oops, did I say transform?

Now that's the "transform" you were expecting! The gorilla turns into a chinchilla. Sure, that's transformation too. We'll get there.

But for now, it's about changing a single behavior.

That's it.

John mentioned in the foreword that in November of 2012 I started writing again. On Day One, I wasn't an award-winning novelist.

I just checked. I wrote utter garbage for most of the those early days. (Have a look for yourself: write-every-day.repossible.com.) But then on Day 26 something seemed to shift.

Something happened in those first 30 days that made me go past the 30 days.

In John's Foreword, I have to admit it: I was offended. He didn't think it was really going to happen. He didn't think this book would exist. What!? Seriously? But if I'm brutally honest with myself, I didn't think it would happen either--I can admit today that I wasn't sure I actually wanted it to happen.

Dreaming the dream was a whole lot easier than living the dream.

No real action, no responsibility, no deadlines, no failure, no effort, no nada. Woo hoo! Let's just keep doing this!

The 2012 Bradley was scared, timid, and had the confidence of a Dik Dik on the open savannah (i.e. shivering with fright of what might happen). Now the 2017 Bradley looks back at that poor sap and thinks, "Seriously? That's what you're worried about? It's nothing. Get over it. C'mon! Step up!"

But I also thank that poor sap. 2012 Bradley took that first step. It was painful, scary, and just plain sucked. Yet, he got past it. He kept going. He didn't know where he was headed, he only knew he needed to keep going. Step away from the unhappiness, lack of focus, and all-around misery.

Dearest reader, my intention for this book is for you to take one tiny step towards the spark that is hiding within you. It might be rough in the beginning. **If you can just get past the slog of the beginning, the magic will start to happen.** I can guarantee it. I don't know which day it will begin. I don't even know if you'll notice that it's happening.

I was miserable. I was depressed. I was an actor living a phony life I didn't want to be in. If you have any of those thoughts, please know there is a way out, but you do have to take a step. That's all I can hope for with this book. One little step.

My fondest desire for you is that this book **motivates your inspiration.**

My "big dream" back in 2012 was to get back into the writing habit. I was pretty sure even that simple goal wasn't going to happen. I'm here today to tell you that dream did come true, and along the way other dreams were born. Bigger, grander dreams I could never have imagined before I started--and would have never discovered had I not started. Had I not taken my first step.

One of my new and deepest rooted dreams is to make an impact in the world, to help people change parts of their lives, to take their hand from the hole they're stuck in and lift them up. Even if I can only lift them high enough to see some light, I know they will get a glimpse of the path for them.

I want you to have what I have. This book is the story of how I got to where I am today. I know I'm not all the way yet, but this is so much better than where I was. If I only got this far, I could live the rest of my life joyously. But now that I'm at this point, I know that there's more.

I want you to know there is always more.

On a purely practical matter, I recommend reading this book in small bursts. Make it a chapter a day or every other day or ... just kidding. I would never recommend anything every other day. Read a chapter per day and if you sneak in some of the lighter or shorter chapters, within a month you'll no longer be where you were on Day Zero.

PART I

PRECAUTION

- prologue: a preface or introductory part of a discourse, poem, or novel
- precaution: a measure taken in advance to avert possible evil or to secure good results
- procrastinate: to defer action; delay; to put off till another day or time;

Normally at the beginning of a book there's a prologue. Nope, not here. "Precaution" is much more appropriate.

Procrastination is going to have to wait until Part 2. (That's a little word humor there. It's OK, you'll get used to it.)

.

1

INTRODUCTION

Vision without action is merely a dream. Action without vision just passes the time. Vision with action can change the world.

— Joel A. Barker

You have a dream. You know it. I know it.

It's OK, I won't tell anyone. It'll be our little secret together as you read this book.

What's the easiest way to keep your dream alive?

Never actually take a step towards it.

"Wait, what?" I hear you get up from your chair and spill your latte. "Aren't we going to crush my fears, achieve my dreams, live my life to the fullest and all that?"

Sure, we can do all that. But I want to give you an out. I don't want you to waste your time with this book if you'd rather just continue to Dream the Dream, but you're not really ready to Live the Dream.

Let me give it to you straight: Dreaming the Dream isn't bad at all. It's like only having dessert at the buffet--but you don't gain weight. It's always your turn at bat--but you never lose the game. It's only dreaming--but you never wake up. Dreaming the Dream is loads of fun. I have extended experience with it: I did it for years ... and years.

If you don't start, you can't fail.

If you don't actually do something about it, then you can continue talking about it at dinner parties and always use the line, "I'm going to start _____ (insert your awesome dream) tomorrow." People will be impressed because you're so action oriented. You can nod your head, beam with pride, have another coconut macaroon from the dessert buffet, and silently know you're still dreaming.

But of course you won't start tomorrow. At tomorrow's dinner party you'll say, yet again, that you'll start tomorrow. You can run into a little trouble if you keep saying this to the same people. They will eventually stop believing or listening or caring--or all of the above.

Solution? Keep going to different dinner parties, of course! Only talk to strangers, and make sure you don't have to actually take action steps towards your dream. That way it's safe and sound where it belongs: only on the comfy sofa of your imagination.

Does this hurt yet? Were those first few paragraphs painful? Oops, did I awaken a bug in your system? Something like a tapeworm that lives within you and eats your insides while you pretend that your life is charmed and focused and intentional?

I'm sorry.

Oops, wait a minute.

Let me rephrase: I'm not sorry.

I'm not sorry because I wish someone had threatened me with such words a decade or so ago.

But no. Back then I kept my dream of being a writer mostly to myself and strangers. Sure it was festering inside of me hoping to be set free. But I squashed it. I didn't let it out. Whew! Lucky me! Good thing, right?

"Keep that dream down there!"

"Hold it down!"

"Lock it up!"

"Don't let it out!"

"That's a stupid idea."

"What a waste of time."

"You're not good enough."

"You're better than that."

"Maybe wait a few decades until you've finished your career."

"It's just not you."

For years, I listened to society and family and friends who all (never actually) said that I should go down a different path, a more logical, rational, and safe path. That my dream was more of a hobby, something to do later in life, more of, well, a dream. Dreams were great for bedtime and story hour at the local library, but not for successful, intelligent, and sensible people.

The problem was the dream wouldn't go away.

I tried. I got degrees. I studied hard. I worked at jobs. I pretended to build a career. From the outside, things looked grand. *I was on top of the world! I had it all! I was living the dream.*

But I wasn't.

Or at least I wasn't living *my* dream.

How long are you going to wait to get started? Do you need some excuses to procrastinate? Doors are opening soon for the Procrastination Workshop. So far, I have 312 tentative sign ups. But no one for certain.

You could wait for a huge life-altering event to really stir things up. I know, wait until your father passes away. Wait for a disease to settle in. Get fired from a job. Quit a job. How about retirement? That's seems rational, right? Ooh, here's one: wait until you're almost dead. Remember the whole afterlife discussion above? Great, we're all set.

But what if you'd like to start soon? Let's pick a day. Ooh, ooh, I know!

Today.

I write these words today as I would have loved to have heard them twenty-six years ago. If someone had forced my hand and told me to take that step in the direction I knew I wanted to go, in the direction I needed to go.

I hope you can take this book today and take the first step towards your dream.

2

THE DEVIL AT THE DINNER PARTY

He who is not everyday conquering some fear has not learned the secret of life.

— Ralph Waldo Emerson

In the last chapter, I briefly mentioned a dinner party. I gloss over it but it pains me to no end to talk about it.

You know how the doctor says, "Now this won't hurt a bit." Yeah, I'm not saying that. This is going to hurt. A lot.

You know when they then say, "This is going to hurt me a lot more than it's going to hurt you." This one is valid. This is going to hurt me to write. You might want to get a coffee--or something stronger.

Here's what I wish with all of my heart had happened at one of those dinner parties many, many years ago. If you don't go to dinner parties, you can also just imagine this when you're home alone and dreaming of a life you're not yet living.

I wish that someone came up to me, maybe at a point when I was really on a roll spilling out all of the glorious fantasies of the life that I was not really yet living. I might have been laughing at the ease of the life I (secretly) didn't have, but I sure knew how to tell it like it was! Or at least, like it might be. I can even see myself raising my glass in a toast to the victories I had not yet won in battles I wasn't even on the battlefield for. But they were all so deliciously marvelous in the ballroom of my imagination.

But then that someone came up to me and gave me a smile and a little nod. He was tall and thick and strong. His smile faded. It was clear that it was a phony smile, like a secret service agent or a captain in the mafia. He had another agenda. I was immediately scared that something was amiss.

Quietly, he took me by the arm--and not exactly gently. I joked to the other guests that I'd be right back. He practically lifted half of my body as he pushed me to a dark and empty corner of the dinner party. He got up into my face. I could smell the alcohol on his breath. Or was that on my breath? I still didn't know what he wanted so I smiled and chuckled and said, "Didn't you get enough of the celery with the spinach dip, my friend?"

I was going to quash this threat by avoiding what he was really after, by making light of the situation, by charming his reality with my fantasies. He said nothing about the spinach dip, but he came even closer to my face so that I could feel the heat from his perspiring brow. He was now definitely no longer smiling.

"How much longer are you going to do it?" he asked in what seemed like a South African accent. But he didn't wait for an answer. His voice came from another place, like it was surround sound.

"When will the day come when the angel on your shoulder walks across your neck to the devil on the other and they make a deal to release your true self that they have locked up deep within the dungeon of your soul?"

His eyes didn't blink. He held my arm and I was pinned to the wall. I had a quick thought that this guy had watched way too many gangster movies. I pretended not to be scared. I wasn't doing a good job. He kept going.

"Or are they going to live separately forever and make you suffer every single day of your life by never coming to a decision to take action, real action, not dinner-party fake chit-chat action, but a single, real, true step towards all of this fluff and dreamy phony future that you rattle on about? That you only talk about but don't experience? That you're so good at imagining and describing about how it all will be but you know nothing of how it actually is?"

He stopped for a minute. The words slithered through my brain like snakes, but snakes with razor blades for scales. The pain in my head was excruciating.

I tried to speak, "But ... "

I had no words. I had no answer. I honestly didn't know what to say to him, what I was supposed to do. I only knew the dream, I didn't know the reality.

"But you don't understand," I said between clenched teeth. If he wanted the truth, fine, I would give it to him. But I was sure, even the tough guy he thought he was, that he couldn't handle it.

"Do tell, dear sir," he mocked in his uppity accent. "Tell me what I don't understand for I know you better than you know yourself." He waited for me to speak, but I was speechless. I was petrified. I wanted more than anything in the world just to go back to the spinach dip.

"You have something inside of you that will eat your insides. You need to set it free. You know what it is. I know what it is. But no one else knows what it is. If you don't let it out, it will fester and infect and spread," he paused. I waited patiently for more torture.

"But I'm going to make it easy on you. I'm going to make it extremely clear. Here's what's going to happen." He paused as if he thought I might tremble and be even more scared than I already was. It worked magnificently. I trembled in my shoes.

"What's going to happen is that every single night, I'm going to come for you. I know where you live, I know where you hang out, I know your every move. I am your nightmare and your devil. I will pin you against walls whenever I feel like it. I will come after you when you think you're safe. Maybe you're on that deck of yours sipping tea alone, like you did last night, and I'll whisper in your ear. I'll be relentless. I will be at your side, on your back, in the shadows of your every waking moment, threatening you, daring you, challenging you, reminding you that you are living a falsehood, a hoax, a dream."

Now he was really annoying. The hatred ballooned from my gut and words came out of my mouth.

"But you don't understand!" I screamed at him. Tears formed in my eyes and my throat was scratchy like after you've vomited multiple times.

"Enlighten me," he whispered in a sweet sounding voice. But with a look that could also gouge my eyes out with the next beat of his heart.

But I couldn't say it. I couldn't admit it. I had never said it out loud, not even in my own head. And now I was supposed to tell my deepest, darkest, most-real-thing-I-knew-in-the-world to this ruffian of a devil in disguise.

"No," I said.

"Tell me," he screamed but in a whisper. If he had a knife, it would have been at my throat.

"I can't," I shouted louder.

"You can," he spoke more quietly.

The tears rolled down my cheeks. I had no more defenses. I was running on empty. I had nothing left but the truth and it was the last thing I could hold onto and if I let go of that, I would fall to the depths of hell.

"I'm scared," I said as quietly as I could.

"Oh, pardon me, my fine gentleman," he said in the snarkiest, meanest tone even the finest actor couldn't have replicated. "What was that?"

Through tears and bile-tasting phlegm I spat out the words.

"I'm scared!"

"Scared of what?" he asked, almost sounding human and caring.

"I'm scared that this is my one and only dream and that if I start and I fail I will have nothing left. Nothing left. Nothing left." I cried through my words as I screamed with a voice I didn't know I had. He said nothing and his gruesome stare became kinder, gentler. Through my tears, I could see his mood lift and he spoke.

"Well, that's the silliest thing I've ever heard," he said and as the words sank into my brain I realized that it was the last thing I would have expected anyone to say.

I wanted to strangle him. I envisioned his eyes popping out as my hands wrapped around his neck. But I couldn't move. He started laughing. I could hardly murder a guy who was laughing.

"What are you laughing at?" I asked as I wiped snot on my sleeve exactly as my youngest son does.

"Why you, of course, my good man," he said in a way too happy tone. "Don't you see the paradox? Don't you comprehend the ridiculousness of it all?"

"No," I said dryly. "I'm afraid I have yet to experience the humor in all of this."

"You have everything you need to make this happen. Don't you see it, my brother?" he looked at me for a response, but I had none. He kept on.

"To turn your colossal mountain range of a dream into a single step on the path."

"A single step?"

"One foot in front of the other," he said and he backed up and off of me, for he had been all of this time practically on top of me. "Let me show you."

He stood with his feet exaggeratedly close to each other.

"Ready?" he asked.

"Uh, yeah," I answered.

"Watch." He lifted his right foot and moved it forward to just a foot's length ahead. "See? Done. Now you try."

I put my feet together with my heels touching the wall he had had me pinned against. I brought my right foot up and forward and placed it on the ground, but carefully, as if the floor were eggshells and I didn't want to break them.

"Was there a Herculean effort there? Did a mountain move? Did you need to part a few seas?"

"Uh, no," I replied timidly.

"Lighten up, man!" he said and slapped me on the shoulder as if we were old college buddies. "It's all a game, don't you see it now?" He stared into me, through me.

"Uh, no," I answered, maybe too honestly.

"You'll get to play later, but there are a few steps to go through first. But you have now taken the first step. Excellent progress, my good chap."

"So are we done here?" I asked, feeling more and more comfortable.

"Not quite," he said not completely unlike the executioner who hadn't quite yet dropped the guillotine on the guilty man.

"We need a schedule," he said matter of factly.

"A schedule?"

"Exactly."

"Like how often I need to take that little step?"

"You're a brilliant student, my brother. Want to take a wild guess as to how often?"

"Every other day plus weekends?" is what came out of my mouth instantly.

"Almost," he whispered like the school teacher who knew your answer was completely wrong. He winked, which completely threw me off. People who wink freak me out.

"Every other day?" I asked, hoping this would work as every other day would also mean a day off in between.

"Just about there," he said, looking at his fingernail.

I knew the answer, but I didn't like it.

"All out of ideas?" he asked.

"No, no," I delayed. "I got it."

"Anytime is good."

"Every single day," I answered.

"Most excellent," he again clasped me on the shoulder. "That's exactly right." He looked at his wrist to check the time, but there was no watch on his wrist.

"I must be moving on," he said. "Quite the roster this evening, you know."

"Uh huh," I said as my brilliant conversational skills kicked into high gear. He didn't ask me if I was OK or ready or say anything else. He just looked at me.

"So," I stuttered.

"Yes?" he drew it out nice and slow and painful.

"That stuff about you lurking in the shadows and pretty much torturing me the rest of my life if I don't take a tiny little step every single day," I paused to make sure he knew what I was talking about. He did.

"So that stuff was all for show, right? I mean, you won't, well, you can't really do that, right? I mean, don't have you other people to torture every night? That won't really happen, right?" I hoped, I prayed even, I clenched my teeth in hopes that he would free me from the persecution that was to haunt me every single day for the rest of my life.

He said nothing. He only gave me a knowing smile.

Then he did something I'll never forget, but can't stand, and wish I could un-see it.

He winked.

3

THE PILL

Give someone who has faith in you a placebo and call it a hair growing pill, anti-nausea pill or whatever, and you will be amazed at how many respond to your therapy.

— BERNIE SIEGEL

There were two pills on the original cover of this book.

I'm a big believer in the power of the placebo, which is the power of the mind. My point with the pills on the cover is to make it seem like I have a "prescription" for change where I'm going to give you a magic pill and your dreams will come true.

Contrarily, if I had put an image of, oh, I don't know, a shovel or an empty road or maybe a barefoot peasant carrying a huge sack of tools on his back slogging up a muddy road towards an insurmountable mountain under the dark clouds of the horizon, you might have been slightly less inclined to want to jump on in and say "Woo hoo! This looks like fun! I'm in! Is that all I have to do to achieve my dreams? Pain and suffering, a heavy burlap sack full of rocks and a long, treacherous road leading to somewhere unknown? Sign me up!"

Humans are wired for simple and easy. So, we're often looking for a magic pill. Believe me, dearest reader, if there had been a pill, with a little butterfly on one side and a cryptic ESD on the other, that I could have taken some long years ago that promised to at least start me on my journey of transformation, that could have possibly made one of my feet move in the slightest direction towards my dream, I would have slipped the shady drug dealer on the corner a $100 bill and swallowed it whole with a chaser of warm Gatorade.

But there was no drug dealer.

In fact, there is no pill.

The pill is ... and don't think I'm giving away the secret of this book somewhere buried here in the introduction ... your mind. No, more precisely, your heart. Sorry, not quite right. The pill is **the overlap of the power of your mind and the passion from your heart to decide what propels you forward to the next step.**

How does that work? How do we get the mind and the heart to work together to fabricate a pill-like environment which converts doubt to certainty, fear to pride, and a dream to reality?

That's what this book is about.

If you'd rather have a pill or a tool or something to lean on to help you, I have that. It's kind of like LSD (the psychedelic drug) and it's even got a little ESP in it (extra sensory perception). It's close to those, but different.

My drug of choice is a little pill called Every Single Day or ESD for short. Except it's not a drug. It's not a pill. There is no actual pill. We could try to create some in a lab, they would be great to hand out at book events, but I don't have a pill. At its core, **the pill represents a decision**: a decision to change a behavior.

You only have to take a little, but there is one recommended dosage: Every Single Day.

More on that later. Let's first get to the Day That Doesn't Count. The Day Before You Start to Count your life in terms of Every Single Day. Let's get to Day Zero.

4

DAY ZERO

What we call the beginning is often the end. And to make an end is to make a beginning. The end is where we start from.

— T. S. ELIOT

I wanted to number this part of the book Part 0. But the book formatting software wouldn't let me. That's because zero doesn't exist for most people. It hasn't really started yet. Nothing begins with Day Zero. There is Day One and then the rest. But it's true, Day Zero doesn't actually exist. Day Zero is an idea, a thought, a potential.

The problem is that most of us live in Day Zero.

You can still escape. If you're not up for the challenge, you can stop reading now and continue on your path--the path in the other direction away from your dream. But I have a tip if you're going to go that way.

Squash that dream now. Throw it on the ground and crush it like a smoldering cigarette butt. Make sure it's good and extinguished so it doesn't come back to haunt you. It will try. It has so much power over you. Put it out of its misery. Or rather, pull its misery out of you.

Now go the other way and run. Run from your dream and live the life someone else suggested you lead. I'll see you later. Or, actually, I won't see you later because I'm going the other way.

If you'd like to join me, come along over to Day One. The first day of your new life. The new direction you'll take when you take that first step towards your dream.

It's a decision you have to make. If you're part of my upcoming Procrastination Workshop you can decide tomorrow. But if you've already taken that course,* you can join us today. Right now. You have to decide. No, truly decide.

Except you have already decided. You know what you want to do, what you need to do. You kept reading after the chapter where I let you escape. You know the path towards your true self and you've been waiting for someone to come along, hold out their hand for yours, and lead you down the path.

Take my hand. I'm heading in that direction anyway. Let's go.

* *That's a joke. No one has actually ever taken the Procrastination Course. Not for lack of interest, but for lack of commitment to starting.*

5

WHO ARE YOU?

Education's purpose is to replace an empty mind with an open one.

— MALCOLM FORBES

O*pen.*
Such a simple word. But packed with a punch.

The only requirement you need to read, finish, and act on what this book has to offer is that you're open to it. You're open to new ideas, new perspectives, directions, and methods. Maybe you're open to a new mindset, a new way of thinking, new habits, new challenges, and new failures.

Oops, did I mention failures? Time for a new chapter.

6

FAILURE

Failure is simply the opportunity to begin again, this time more intelligently.

— HENRY FORD

The only failure I now know is the failure to give something a shot. The failure to start, to launch, to take a step.

From my perspective, there is no failure, there is only learning from mistakes. In fact, I've learned that we learn more from failure than from success. My son makes the shot in basketball and thinks he no longer needs to practice. He misses and then he needs to adjust his stance, his hands, and the power of release.

Failure means I'm trying. An advanced skier told me that if I didn't fall at least once per day on the slopes, I wasn't pushing myself hard enough, I wasn't learning, I wasn't advancing.

Huh? By failing I'm advancing? It went against all of my logic.

But please, go with it. Be open to it. Fail and fail often. Fail small and keep at it. Soon it will simply be a part of your day. Want to know the best part? Failure will no longer bother you.

Did you catch that?

Failure will no longer bother you. Let that sink in. It's a big deal.

Someday, you'll fail yet again, think of this chapter, smile, and keep at it.

7

POSSIBLE, IMPOSSIBLE, REPOSSIBLE

The difference between the impossible and the possible lies in a man's determination.

— TOMMY LASORDA

What do you believe is possible? What do you believe is impossible? What do you believe is possible for you? What do you believe is impossible for you?

Do you believe that your dream, your passion, your goal, your whatever-you-want-to-call it, is possible or impossible?

I no longer see possible and impossible as black and white, yes or no, zeros and ones. There is a third path. A method, a mindset, that finds another way around impossible and yet slides by the possible. It's not necessarily better or worse, smarter, better, but it's from another perspective, from a new perspective.

It's a mindset, a philosophy, a meaning. I use the term Repossible when the answer isn't so cut and dried, where I need a new take on the challenge to see another way in--or out. It's OK to move the goalposts, change the rules of the game. It's OK to change the game.

At the end of each chapter, I'll end with three bullet points:

- Possible:
- Impossible:
- Repossible:

Here are the quick descriptions of those terms:

- Possible: the hard way
- Impossible: the easy way
- Repossible: your way

I try to, in the fewest words I can muster, summarize each chapter by showing the easy way, the hard way and your way. Call it what you will: the best way, the smart way, the efficient way, the effective way. You get the idea.

Here's what I really think about each point.

Possible

Start by doing what's necessary; then do what's possible; and suddenly you are doing the impossible.

— FRANCIS OF ASSISI

The hard way.

This is usually the way we think it needs to happen. It's seems contradictory, but the Possible way is what we think of as the Easy Way, but it's usually the Hard Way. Possible involves ideas like: going it alone, hard work, slow, chaotic, etc.

This way isn't necessarily wrong, but it's the slow way. With Possible, I see it as the way to keep the status quo, to stay where you are, not advance or maybe only advance slowly and surely. But feel "good" doing it because you're "working hard" at it.

You'll get there eventually. Well, probably. This is the thick-headed method, the I-can-do-it-and-you-can-try-to-stop-me approach that will get you somewhere, maybe nowhere, but not really where you want to go.

When you're not sure what to do, take the Possible route to get from A to B. But C? Maybe C is Repossible.

Impossible

> Progress is impossible without change, and those who cannot change their minds cannot change anything.
>
> — GEORGE BERNARD SHAW

The easy way.

It might not be necessarily cheating, but it's a shortcut. Just like a "sugar free, diet chocolate cake." C'mon, seriously?

It's also unrealistic. This would be "Dreaming the Dream" instead of "Living the Dream." It sounds good at dinner parties, it looks good on paper, but you know (and it might be your little secret) that it's not really going to work.

I completely realize that these might seem contradictory or that they're even mislabeled. Call them or label them as you like. One is easy, one is hard. They both usually don't really work or at least get you to where you truly are headed.

Repossible

> Everything should be made as simple as possible, but not simpler.
>
> — ALBERT EINSTEIN

Your way.

Repossible changes the rules. Repossible might even change the game. Repossible is a different perspective from where you see different challenges and even different goals.

If Possible is walking straight ahead from the junction in the middle of the desert and Impossible is refusing to go anywhere, sitting down in the dust in a pout and waiting for someone to come pick you up, then Repossible is looking around, seeing things with fresh perspective, and realizing that there is a drinking fountain that just rose up out of a mirage. With sparkling water.

Repossible, yes, it's true, has a sense of humor.

Repossible, and I'm not sure how else to say this, doesn't really care so much about the other two guys in the desert: Possible and Impossible. He's not on their team. He's not in their league. He doesn't even play the same game.

Repossible is taking a step up and seeing things from a higher plane.

I'm going to leave it at that.

For now.

8

YOU, ME, AND FOUR OTHERS

Don't wait to be successful at some future point. Have a successful relationship with the present moment and be fully present in whatever you are doing. That is success.

— ECKHART TOLLE

I see this book as a conversation. A relaxed, usually calm conversation between you and me. Between the me of the past, present, and future and the you of the past, present, and future. Yeah, that's going to be six people. We might want to set up a conference call.

I want it to be conversational, easy going, and relatable. I want the me of the past, present, and future to relate to one or all of the you personas from the past, present, and future.

Well, honestly, I care less about the you or me of the past. It's history, done, can't change that. The future you is what we're creating with the you of the present.

In fact, we only truly have the present. The future you depends on the present you. It's the present you I'm interested in talking with. It's the present me talking with the present you that's going to make for the most enlightening of chats.

So hi there! My name is Bradley. Ready for the ride?

- Possible: past
- Impossible: future
- Repossible: present

PART II

PROCRASTINATION

JUST START THIS PART TOMORROW.

9

INTRODUCTION

Procrastination is one of the most common and deadliest of diseases and its toll on success and happiness is heavy.

— WAYNE GRETZKY

I f you don't water the plants until tomorrow, they'll survive.

If you don't feed the dog until the weekend, he'll probably live. He'll even wag his tail and love you next week (if he survived the weekend of course).

If you don't take a stab at giving your dream a chance, if you keep putting it off until things are just right, until this project is completed and that task is taken care of ... if you talk about your dream with friends as if you're going to start any day now, but never do ... if you go into long conversations with strangers on airplanes about your thoroughly researched plans for your dream future but you get off the plane and never speak of it ... if you think that "someday" will come ... if you wish and want and plead and pray, but take no action ... if you keep it all bottled up inside and never let it out ... if you think someone will come along one day and ask if you're ready to begin day one of your dream ... if you're waiting ... if you're pretending ... if you're living the life you know is not the truest version of you ... if you don't take the first step, if you don't give your dream a chance, at least a peek outside of its tightly-closed prison cell ... if you don't start.

Whew. Heavy! Yeah, sorry. OK, I'm not sorry.

Still, let's lighten things up.

Procrastination is when you walk by the loose screw in the door hinge 87 times and each time think about it, say to yourself that you're going to fix it, kick yourself that you don't do it, even tell your wife that you'll do it, still don't do it, then finally, one day, seemingly spur of the moment, you fix it on the 88th time. You just spent one hour and eleven minutes of your life not doing the thing and then you do the thing and it took less than two minutes to finish (get screwdriver, make four good turns, done).

That was light. Now we can go back to heavy.

I gave you a chance in the beginning of this book to opt out, to stop reading, to keep Dreaming the Dream--but not actually Living the Dream. But if you're this far, if you're still reading, then the dream inside of you is alive and ... (maybe not so) well.

I didn't mention this little tidbit of horror in the first chapter, but there are consequences to keeping that dream bottled up inside you. They are nasty, real, and nowhere near fun. If you're not ready to get real, you can just lounge around in the Procrastination section and hang out there for a decade or two like I did. Here's what happens if you never take action towards living your dream.

It will eat away at you. It will rot your insides. If you never let it see the light of day, it will fester and bloom, but will only thrive inside of you until it's like a tumor. At some point in your life there will be less room for other important bodily functions and you will begin to suffer physically, emotionally, and psychologically. It will make food taste less good. It will make your daily life seem worthless or less important which will lead to you feeling worthless or less important.

At the end of each day you might fall asleep to the nightmare that you didn't take any action towards your dream and wake up with the threat that you might do the same thing again.

I suppose that, after an extremely long time, if you don't ever, ever let it out of its cage, it will, possibly, slowly die. It's possible that it might go away completely.

Can you ever get it back? I don't know about this scenario but for me, it never went away. But maybe it's possible. Death of your unlived dream might sound like a good thing, except this isn't something you want to get rid of, it's something you need and desperately want to keep working. This thing is your heart.

Maybe in your next life, if you believe in that sort of thing, you'll be able to live your dream. Maybe if you're a cat. Otherwise, we only have one life in this body on this planet and it's now or never. Well, or we can start tomorrow. Or never. The good news and the bad news is that the choice is completely our own.

It's good news because we can decide to take a stand and take a step towards our dream.

It's bad news because we can choose not to. Or we can choose to procrastinate.

I don't know if this will all happen to you. But it happened to me.

Then one day, I turned around and started walking the other way.

"What!?" I hear you again stand up, this book still in your hand, staring incredulously at the words, your popcorn spilled all over the floor. "Well, that sure sounded easy. Why didn't you just do that before?" You talk to the book. Then I hear you whisper to yourself, "Dang, this guy is a slow learner." But you read on.

Because that first step was the biggest, nastiest, and most difficult step in my life.

That step was in the direction of my dream and I knew I couldn't turn back. I wasn't ready. I was scared to a level that I had rarely, if ever, experienced because **you can only be truly scared of the things you care about.**

I took the first step.

That was in 2012.

That seems like ages ago now. But the time before that was longer. Much longer. Eternity-style, waiting-at-the-post-office-and-then-they-close longer.

Procrastination time is slow time. You know that setting on your camera that captures life in slow motion? Procrastination is living in that mode. It's torturous, it's slow. It's slow torture.

But when you break free from its grasp, it switches to regular video mode. You step off of the treadmill or the sand dune to a place where each step forward doesn't equal one (or two) steps back. You move forward in real time.

Let's get there.

10

THE PERFECT STORM

One life is all we have and we live it as we believe in living it. But to sacrifice what you are and to live without belief, that is a fate more terrible than dying.

— JOAN OF ARC

People I meet these days have little to no idea the path that brought me to where I am today. When they ask what I do, I say, "I'm an author." It took me 26 years to get to this point. Here's what happened. This is the condensed version, I swear.

Back in 1990, I sat alone in a library in Amsterdam and wrote stories. With a pen. In a little notebook. I was pretty sure I wanted to be a writer. I'm pretty sure there was thunder and lightning in my soul. *Apparently, the storm bypassed the heart of the city.*

At highway rest stops after work at my corporate consulting job in 1996, I sat in my car and wrote stories on my laptop. *Clouds in the distance.*

I joined a writer's group in San Francisco when we moved there in 2000. We helped Khaled Hosseini work on drafts of what would later become "The Kite Runner." My dream was alive, but more like kindling, the fire not yet quite burning. *Cloudy with a chance of occasional showers.*

For some masochistic reason, I chose not to write myself, but set up a company to help writers with their marketing strategies starting around 2006. It was being the waterboy for the basketball team. Sure, you were a "part of the industry" but you weren't a player. *Forecast? Overcast with little chance of light.*

On November 1, 2012, I accepted an "experiment" to write Every Single Day from a friend who was running Monthly Experiment workshops: the slave driver, I mean, my dear friend John Muldoon whom you met in the foreword. You'd think this would have kicked my writing career into gear. You'd think. I enjoyed that day job of helping other writers less and less. I shouldn't even have "enjoy" and "day job" and "I" in the same sentence. I was miserable, desperate. *Rumbling in the distance. Clouds formed. Slowly.*

In 2013, I was not-really-diagnosed with something that might eventually turn into something else. Fear, panic, depression. "I know, let's imagine the worst possible outcome! I'll probably die next month!" I kept writing. I searched for help. I needed to write to keep me sane and quell the fear. I discovered meditation. *Shivers of thunder in the distance. Faint sparks of lightning.*

In March of 2014 while sitting on the big red chair in the living room, my son and I read a bad children's book. "We can do better than that," I said. I happened to notice that the last book I had published was a travel guidebook for San Francisco. The date of that book was April 1, 2004. It sent a shiver down my spine--and not the good-feeling kind. We published "The Secret of Kite Hill" less than a month later, on April 1, 2014. *A crackle of thunder in the hills in the distance. The storm was brewing.*

2015 brought the passing of my father. This wasn't supposed to happen to me, to my family. He had so much left to give, to love, to experience. I wasn't done with him being in my life. This wasn't how my life was supposed to go. In fact, my **life just kept going as it had been going because no one was doing anything to change it.** My father's passing opened my eyes to mortality. I delved deeper into my writing and meditation. I hit 1,000 posts in 1,000 days. I wrote two more children's books together with my sons. *Boom. I heard it in the distance. The kind of thunder that rattles your insides. It was nearby.*

In 2016, my wife and I packed up four suitcases and moved to her home country: The Netherlands. I barely had a business left to leave. I left my business waving at me from the proverbial ship's deck. It was crying. I was not. I could move on. I kept writing. Another children's book. I started writing non-children's fiction. *Thunder crashed into my heart. Lightning was so close I could practically feel it.*

There were no more excuses. "Procrastination" itself was tired of procrastinating. The planets aligned, 26 years had passed since I sat alone in a library in Amsterdam scribbling stories, dreaming that one day I might be an actual writer.

In 2017, I've written four short works of fiction, started a (secret ... ok, formerly secret: https://goo.gl/LZmKHX) podcast, and wrote, published, and marketed the book you're holding in your hands. There is no way anyone can say I'm not a writer. It's taken me this long to get here and there is no turning back. I'm a turtle, a tank, I'm slow, I'm unstoppable, determined, and fierce. *The storm has arrived. I am the storm.*

That's procrastination at its finest. One of my goals with this book is to cut 26 years down to something a little more manageable for you.

Let's get going with that, shall we?

- Possible: wait out the storm
- Impossible: predict the weather
- Repossible: be the storm

11

PURGATORY

If you're going through hell, keep going.

— WINSTON CHURCHILL

In keeping with the Casual Conversation style of this book, I'm going to occasionally let you in on some of the behind the scenes workings of the machine.

In working on the title for this section of the book that started with the letter P, there were just so many juicy options:

- pain
- paralysis
- pause
- postpone
- prolong
- puke
- put off
- passive

Are we having fun yet?

It would be quite the attention grabber, but I just couldn't use Puke as the section title although it's the one that hits home the most. Prolong is annoying, but also passive.

Procrastination, if you're procrastinating about something important, can be extremely painful and induce some serious puking. You can try to postpone the paralysis, but you're probably too passive to put it off. So just puke because you're sick to your stomach because you haven't lived your dream life, you haven't even started it. In fact, your dream life is just that: a dream. Pause.

Purge. Permit. Purify.

You can now proceed, progress, and prosper.

Pleased?

- Possible: permit
- Impossible: predict
- Repossible: stick to section headings that start with the letter "p" even if it drives you ... psycho

12

YOU KNOW THOSE THINGS YOU NEVER SEEM TO GET DONE?

Procrastination is the thief of time.

— EDWARD YOUNG

Y ou spend months thinking about doing something and then you finally do it and it takes only minutes? Loose screw in door hinge?

Yeah, you won't have those anymore.

It's a mathematical challenge beyond the greatest minds in the field. Something that ends up taking only minutes, yet there are hours, even days and weeks spent in the build up. Remember, we're not talking about something that you need to train for (e.g. a marathon), or maybe something that's crazy important (e.g. your PhD dissertation), we're talking about do-able, finish-able things.

But in your mind, they're often huge, possibly even insurmountable and plain annoying.

When you take ESD, stuff gets done.

Whatever it is you choose to do (or rather, whatever chooses you ... but that's another conversation), you will get it done because you are committed, determined, and will stop at nothing to Get It Done.

You do it Every Single Day so just put it on the ESD Conveyor Belt™ and it will get done.

Dear non-ESDers, I understand that probably sounds overly simplified. But it is simple. Just maybe not easy at first. Later on we'll cover how it can be both simple and easy, but for now, let's just stick with simple.

It's also highly contagious.

In case the door hinge didn't convince you ... I've spent the last, oh, two months not putting up blinds in my son's room. It's now May and it's sunny so early in the morning and so late in the evening you'd think we live in Greenland. The blinds sat on the floor of his room all this time. We tripped over them, cursed them, and wondered why they hadn't been magically installed onto the windows.

Then yesterday, it happened. We put one up. Now we're putting up the others. It took about 15 minutes and it was done.

How can that be possible? How can we expend so much energy not doing something when it only takes a fraction of energy to get it done?

BONUS: when you get it done, you no longer spend any energy on it.

DOUBLE BONUS: you earn or gain energy because of the pride of accomplishment you feel. Not to mention the joy and relief that pours over you for having gotten it off of your plate--or your floor. You walk by those blinds and they practically inject adrenaline into your veins.

It's weird math and science, but it's simple. Later, we'll work on easy. Stay tuned.

But for now: banish procrastination and listen to the Nike ad men: Just Do It.

- Possible: do it tomorrow
- Impossible: do it yesterday
- Repossible: do it today

13

THE CONUNDRUM OF COMFORTABLE

I'm not interested in preserving the status quo; I want to overthrow it.

— NICCOLO MACHIAVELLI

We're about to enter the choppy waters of Part 3: Passion. There's just one more chapter first, I promise. It's the perfect ending to the Procrastination section: "No, I'm not ready yet! Just one more thing!"

You often hear the heart-torturing stories of someone who has come back from the depths of hell to rise up and go above and beyond where they started.

Samantha had always dreamt of being a professional bowler, but her house had just been swept away by the avalanche (only the bowling balls remained -- a sign!?).

Her husband was kidnapped by evildoers.

Her job at the accountancy agency dangled by a thread.

Her doctor hinted that she might want to "get her affairs in order."

She struggled, she cried herself to sleep, she fought, she climbed, she ascended, and finally there she was, dirt in between her teeth, a dead cockroach in her hair, but she was at the summit and was beaming, glowing, at the top of her life and there was pounding music and fireworks and it was all glorious. She did it! She truly, actually did it.

When she declared in a Facebook post that she was leaving the accountancy and going after her passion to go pro in bowling, the virtual crowds lifted her up on their virtual shoulders and paraded her through the virtual streets. She was on cloud nine. Everyone understood that after all of the torture and torment and terrible tragedy, this was a clear path to redemption. They applauded her bold move and the calls started coming in from talk shows for her to tell her story.

Then there's Fred. Fred actually sat in a cubicle near Samantha at the accountancy, but they were not close friends. Samantha was probably going to get fired, but Fred's job was safe. In fact, Fred's whole life was safe. His house was on the hill, so it didn't get swept away. He was in pretty good health, at least that's what his routine check-up said. He wasn't really into bowling, but every single night on his drive home from work he dreamt of following his true, deep and pure passion: Macramé.

He'd only told a few strangers, usually on airplanes, about his dream because he thought most people would think he was crazy. He'd done extensive research and was rather certain that there was a hole in the market for the variant called Cavandoli macramé. He had a secret business plan hidden in the bottom drawer of the bathroom, under the extra cotton balls. He even went so far as to meet with a business strategist about his idea and the strategist said, verbatim, "Fred, you're hiding a goldmine here. Based on your numbers and your passion, you'd be an idiot not to pursue this dream of yours. Oh, and if you don't do it, I might just do it myself. No offense."

But the accountancy needed him. He'd been there for seven years and he had good healthcare benefits and they had those everything bagels that were somehow toasted just right--he could never replicate that at home as much as he tried.

He had conversations with himself on those long drives home at night. "Everyone would make fun of me. I mean, seriously, who does macramé? And then Cavandoli macramé? It sounds like an Italian yoga pose."

Every Single Night he tortured his soul in the silence and solitude of freeway traffic. Other than this "cute little side dream" of his, his life was perfect: a solid job with a good income, a perfect family life, a dog, they traveled to kind-of-exotic places on holiday, he even just bought a new weed whacker and when he wore his noise-cancelling headphones, the sound was blocked out and he could whack weeds in the garden and listen to his favorite podcast, "Machiavellian Macramé Master Class." It was only 45 minutes and if he really got every corner of the garden meticulously, he could hear an entire episode. It was pure bliss.

Fred was torn up inside. On the outside, his life was just fine. It was as it should be. On the inside, it was (WARNING: here comes a word that you might want to shield your eyes from): comfortable.

Like a tar pit that slowly kept even the strongest of dinosaurs stuck in its sticky morass. Or a sand hill that was worse than two steps forward and one step back and it wasn't even one step forward and two steps back. No no. This was the ultimate in torture: **this sand hill where Fred parked his life was one step forward and one step back.**

It was a Groundhog Day of an existence. He secretly hoped he might get fired. When he heard about Samantha's house getting swept away in the flood, he quietly accepted that his house was fine and he could continue on with the status quo--but why didn't he buy on the lower part of the hill? Maybe that would have been **the trigger that allowed his life to change.**

He waited, extremely patiently for some external force to sweep in and make that change. He even kept an eye out for it and would have welcomed it with open arms--even if it meant no more everything bagels.

But it never came.

As he drove home on yet another night in traffic, he wondered if that big external change would ever come. He turned up the volume on his podcast and slumped down **in the driver's seat.**

Who has it better off? Whose struggles are more "real"? Who are you? Who's in the driver's seat?

- Possible: Fred
- Impossible: Samantha
- Repossible: You

Overheard on the Street

- "Yeah, my relationship is abusive, but it's not that abusive."
- "I know, I know, I'll get there. I'm just waiting for that little nudge to push me over the edge."
- "Well, it's easy for you. Your dad died."
- "I don't have time."
- "I'm not you."
- "Maybe I'll start next year."
- "I'm going to retire in six years, I'll think about it then."
- "Dude, I'm Fred. You wrote about me?"

PART III

PASSION

INTRODUCTION

Passion is energy. Feel the power that comes from focusing on what excites you.

— OPRAH WINFREY

Of the sections of this book, Passion is either the easiest or the hardest.

It's the easiest if it's crystal clear what your passion is. It's also fairly easy if you have no idea: because you can figure it out.

It's the hardest if you think you know, but you're doubting.

Either way, it is terribly important. Vitally important.

Think of the solar system. If you were to send an unmanned rocket to Jupiter, you'd set the coordinates just so, calculating distance and speed of the rotation of the earth and whatnot. But if you got the trajectory just a little bit wrong, you might end up on Mars. Bit of a problem for the rocket. Thankfully, what you're doing is less scientific--but no less important.

If your dream is to become a pianist but after a year you decide that it was actually, truly, and deep down that you wanted to become a hedge fund manager, it's probably not too late. Or you'd like to lose a little weight. You want to stop biting your nails. Stop drinking. Take up Cavandoli macramé (I know a guy ...). Quit your job. *Keep* your job. Write a book. Compose music. You get the idea.

More important than trajectory is lift off.

You just need to get started.

It's honestly as simple as that.

I think I experienced both the good news and the bad news of Passion at the same time. I knew exactly what my dream was yet at the same time, I didn't pursue it.

Like that darling tapeworm mentioned previously, it ate me up for years, decades even. How come if I knew my dream, I knew what my passion was, that I didn't act on it? Oops, did we skip the chapters on Procrastination? Procrastination knows no end. Passion can also sit and fester. Together with Procrastination. In fact, I bet they're big pals. I think they hang out inside of your head and laugh at how we think it's one or the other and they continue laughing together knowing it's a combination of both of them.

If you're still a little on the fence about what exactly it means, Passion, we can fix that.

If you say that you don't know what yours is, I understand. But if you say that you have no big dream that you are passionate about, then I believe you less.

I believe that we were all born with dreams and passions and imaginations and creativity, but that our external world gnaws at them, grinds them down, and can even bury them so deep that we have trouble finding them or even believing that we have them.

If you're struggling to find your passion, think about what gives you energy. What do you do that you seem to do effortlessly? What makes time fly? What do you look forward to doing more of as soon as you finish doing it? What makes you smile? What do you raise your hand to volunteer for? What gives you goosebumps?

Please note, if this wasn't clear yet, this book is not "Find your Passion and Make a Million Dollars." You'll see by Part 6 that there are things ultimately more important (and fun and rewarding) than financial gain. Sure, chances are good that it'll happen, but it's more of a Side Effect than a result.

The Passion I'm after goes deeper. I'm much more interested in you finding your joy, your happiness, your worth, your value, your freedom, your peace, your addition to the world. I don't believe that you'll do that by doing something you don't love. Sure, it's possible, but why bother? Yes, to pay the bills. I get that part. Important, too. But this is beyond bills.

Here's a test. **Go talk to someone over the age of 80.** Ask them what Passion is. Ask them what they regretted that they never did or didn't do enough of. What were they happy they did? What are their memories about? What makes them happy now that made them happy then? If they don't answer, ask them again. It's there, you might have to dig a little.

If you can't find your answer with them or at least a better definition of what Passion means for you, imagine yourself beyond 80 years old.

You're sitting on a porch overlooking a lake, a glass of iced tea in your hand. You have a few minutes to yourself and you have a quick glance back over your life. You think about some of the things you did that made you most proud. The things that, at 80+ years old on that porch, still bring a tear to your eye and a shiver down your spine, the hair on your neck stand up and a smile that you can't deny.

You might get choked up because you're so emotional that you can't talk about it. But you will talk about it because it's who you became--or didn't become. It's not just what you did, it's who you were--or hopefully who you are even at 80+. What you choose to do or not do today is possibly that first step to the hairs standing up on your neck when you're on that porch with the iced tea.

That's what I'm after. But I'm after it today. Not when I'm 80.
Today.

- Possible: love
- Impossible: hate
- Repossible: passion

15

HOW DO YOU KNOW IF YOU'RE READY TO MAKE "THE LEAP"?

All growth is a leap in the dark, a spontaneous unpremeditated act without benefit of experience.

— HENRY MILLER

Remember the rocket? Scary, right? If you're concerned that you're going to head off into the wrong trajectory, just stop that thinking right now. Feel better?

It's much more important to take action, take a step, make the leap.

Pardon me for I know I just mentioned "take a step" and then "make the leap" in the same sentence. In a way, they're the same at the point where we are now (which is, by the way, the very beginning). But the small step, the tiny little movement of a toe in a the direction of your dream is the equivalent of a huge leap to you.

"That's one small step for [a] man, one giant leap for mankind." -- Neil Armstrong

The secret to this step is just that: it can be miniscule. It can be barely discernible. At this point, it might even be a thought or a change of thought. You might just switch a tiny place in your brain where you used to say "No way." and now you say "Maybe."

The Passion is there. We know that. Check. But it's allowing it to surface. The tiny step, the leap, might be as seemingly insignificant as allowing it to surface, succumbing to the years that it has plagued you, allowing it to exist.

Maybe "The Leap" is a different chapter for you. Maybe it could be called "The Push." I was dragged unwillingly into a 30-Day Experiment to Write Every Day that scared me so much I was sick to my stomach. Maybe we all need that push--or pull. Maybe we don't need it. Maybe we know we're ready.

A friend pointed me to a podcast about people who make Big Changes in their lives. Have a listen to The Leap: Episode 4: The Improbable Transformation of a Punk Pioneer (https://goo.gl/ZW-p6Qp). Here's an excerpt:

> "So now that I'm working on this podcast about people who make dramatic changes, I'm starting to realize something about them. Many people who leap are not agonizers. They don't spend a lot of time considering the other hand, they're not crippled by regrets. And I just don't get that because I'm a regretter and for me there is always another hand to worry over, which is probably why I've never played guitar in a genre-breaking band or became a tech executive."
>
> — JUDY CAMPBELL OF THE LEAP

I think we're safe to sum it up as a "gut feeling." It's much more a decision of the heart over one of the mind. It's not necessarily rational and it might seem crazy to others and downright insane to those who don't understand.

Do you feel it enough to make the leap? What if we just renamed "The Leap" to "A Tiny Little Shuffle of My Big Toe?"

- Possible: step

- Impossible: leap
- Repossible: move forward

16

YOU DO IT EVEN WHEN YOU DON'T WANT TO.

Passion is one great force that unleashes creativity, because if you're passionate about something, then you're more willing to take risks.

— YO-YO MA

Y ou do it even when you don't think it's helping. You do it when you are pretty certain it's a complete waste of time. You do it when no one is watching, when no one cares, and you're not even sure if you still care.

But you do.

So you do it.

I'm coming across more and more ESDers who do what they do Every Single Day because it has become who they are. There are:

1. Writers who write Every Single Day,
2. Business owners who meditate Every Single Day,
3. Athletes who train Every Single Day.

They know they don't need to do it every day. If they missed a day, they are bothered, but it won't break them, but they won't miss two--

and they probably even try to make up for the day they missed even though they know it doesn't really matter.

It's a choice. You choose to whine or you choose to improve.

Sometimes, they don't feel like it. Sometimes they think it's not helping. Maybe they think it was all a big waste of time and they're heading down the wrong path. Occasionally they doubt what they're doing. Maybe they even doubt who they are. But they keep doing it.

It's so much more than "do." You might say that they do it because they "believe." But at some point, the "do" turns into "believe" and at some point it becomes "know." They're not just guessing that it's working, they know. They might not even be able to prove it or do a PowerPoint presentation on it, but they also don't need to. It becomes something that they no longer need to prove to anyone else because it's bigger than that.

Maybe I don't feel like it. Maybe I don't want to. Maybe I think I'm wasting my time and it's all been just a big mirage. Maybe I doubt. Maybe.

Early on in the Passion phase, ESDers like to hear about other people who would rather do something else because it reduces the competition. Later on, true ESDers think more about cooperation and even cultivation over competition.

The passion needs to be larger than doubt. When you dig down into your heart and you see the two battling it out, who wins? The passion or the doubt?

It might not be over in a single battle. It's the war we're interested in. Stay strong.

- Possible: want
- Impossible: should
- Repossible: must

17

I MOTIVATED HIM TO START. HE WAS INSPIRED TO STAY.

People often say that motivation doesn't last. Well, neither does bathing - that's why we recommend it daily.

— ZIG ZIGLAR

Y ou can't force inspiration. But you can force motivation which can lead to inspiration.

You can push or you can be pulled.

I pretty much forced my son into a four-day intensive basketball camp.

"You'll like it, I promise," I told him, knowing how much he loves basketball. He is coordinated and has some talent, but he's not a big believer in practice. Or physical activity.

"It's vacation; I want to chill."

"Chill means doing absolutely nothing in front of a screen," I replied.

"Exactly," he said with pride that dad understood.

"It'll be fun. You want to have some fun."

"I'm not going."

"You'll love it."

"I'll hate it."

"You're going."

He wasn't thrilled to say the least. But he succumbed. And after day three, after eight hours on the court just that one day, we couldn't get him off.

That's motivation transforming into inspiration.

Let's define a few terms:

> *Motivate: to provide with a motive, or a cause or reason to act; incite; impel*

> *Inspire: to fill with an animating, quickening, or exalting influence; to communicate or suggest by a divine or supernatural influence*

Motivation is sweat and pushing.

Inspiration is sweet and pulling.

Motivation is what you do until you are inspired.

What can you do about it today? How can you get inspired? Motivate. What's the only thing you have control over? Motivation. What are you hoping to achieve? Inspiration.

Go to the basketball camp even if you don't want to. Be inspired through your motivation. Get better because you're there, because you want to, you're trying to. At some point, the shift will tilt in your direction and you'll be able to stop pushing and start enjoying the pull of something greater. That's inspiration. It will come. Be persistent, patient, and passionate.

- Possible: motivate
- Impossible: inspire from thin air
- Repossible: motivate to inspire

18

THE ONLY PRODUCTIVITY TIP YOU'LL EVER NEED.

I wake up very early in the morning. I like to start in the dark, and I never work at night, because my brain is evaporated by 4 P.M.

— ALICE SEBOLD

I f you haven't woken up to this productivity tip, you're asleep at the wheel.

(That's a little productivity humor from a morning person. The rib-tickling comedy will grow on you. Keep reading.)

It doesn't matter what you're looking to improve in:

- Making more money,
- Getting healthier or more fit,
- Making the basketball team,
- Being happier,
- Writing a spectacular novel,
- Changing directions in your life,
- Losing weight.

It's just one trick and you're better off. It's also not mutually exclusive. Meaning that if you use this technique you can still use other techniques. In fact, I encourage it. This will be the basis for all other techniques and eventually those other methods will fall away after they've done their job.

This isn't a job or a task or even really a trick--except in the sense that it's something like magic. If you cringe the first time you hear it, it's OK, it will get easier.

If it makes you feel better, you can pay me $97 for letting you in on the secret. Or we could have eight weekly phone calls over two months. Or I could write a book and cite sources and research and experts. If I do it that way, you might actually believe me more. It might soak deeper into your core and you'll more quickly adapt to the new life you've created.

But I don't have time for all of that. Here we are in a chapter of the book and let's just get this over with. I'm just going to tell you the big secret.

Ready? Don't cringe. Don't panic. Don't run. Let it soak in.

Wake up earlier.

I didn't even bold it. Part of that was so that people didn't read ahead through all of my dramatic build up to something so painfully easy it sounds easily painful.

There are deeper additional instructions on top of just waking up earlier,* but for now, know that it's as simple as this. I challenge you, without giving you any more advisement on what to actually do with that extra time in the morning, to set the alarm one hour earlier than normal and simply work on a practical aspect of striving towards your goal or dream.

If you just can't figure out how to get that extra hour in the morning, take it in the evening. Kids in bed, dishes washed, ready? Make it your hour.

Sounds simple, right?

That's because it is.

*I'm just kidding about the deeper instructions. There are no "deeper *instructions." One of the tools of ESDers is finding more time in the day and I just gave you the key to the secret antechamber. Boom. Just like that.*

- Possible: sleep
- Impossible: sleep work (like sleep walking, but working)
- Repossible: wake up

19

WHAT IF YOU HAD ONE DECISION LESS TO MAKE EVERY SINGLE DAY?

Sometimes you make the right decision, sometimes you make the decision right.

— PHIL MCGRAW

How many decisions do we make on a daily basis? What if we subtracted just one?

But we did it Every Single Day?

That would be 30 fewer decisions per month, 365 fewer per year. Think of the extra time, energy, and focus you will have. Not *would* have but *will* have.

Did you catch that? You just made one decision less.

It's not whether or not you're going to do something because you've now got that covered. It might be when you'll do it in the day, but that's such a small decision and not an "if" decision but a "when" decision and those are details.

Once you decide that you're going to join the ESD Movement, you'll be dissecting a part of your brain and tossing it in the recycling. You'll have one less decision, one big decision less per day, every day.

ESD > TEOD

You no longer have to think about if you're going to do it at all today or debate with yourself whether today or tomorrow is better. If yesterday you really should have, but didn't, and then since you didn't do it yet today you'll do double time later today, but by later today you're no longer really sure when you did it the day before yesterday and whether or not that still counts as Twice Every Other Day or even Once Every Third Day and if making up twice on the second and a half day, you'll soon not only be convinced that Every Single Day is simpler than Twice Every Other Day (TEOD) but you'll be yearning for it.

If the theoretical case above isn't clear enough, here's a Real World example.

Let's find a test case. Anyone? Anyone? Hmm. OK, fine: me.

On November 1, 2012, a decision was made for me when I started a 30-Day Experiment to Write Every Day for 30 days. Well, OK, I agreed, but reluctantly. I didn't really want to start down a path because I wasn't sure what was going to happen, if I could really do it, and I thought I might fail miserably. I was just plain scared.

Scared of failure and deeper down and I wouldn't have admitted it but possibly scared of success. It was all just safer to talk about and not actually truly do. Sheesh, that sounds like reasons enough to Just Don't Do It, right?

I should mention at this point that we're talking about a tough decision, one that you don't take lightly and in fact, you'd rather not make at all because it will have more to do with who you become than what you're doing Every Single Day.

There's a factor, a power, a deeper force at play here because you know that you actually can't not do this thing you're lamenting, that you're hemming and hawing about, that you just can't decide to do or not. I get it. I've been there. I didn't want to start either. Because starting opens you to failure.

If you don't start, you can't lose.

Well, sorry, but you can.

Only if you start, can you progress, can you turn your Once In A While decision into an Every Single Day mantra that you live by. That annoying little guy on one of your shoulders will be obliterated by the angel with the tattoo on the other shoulder who takes over and has made that decision for you. It's now done. It's no longer a decision, but a part of what you do and soon it will be a part of who you are.

I know: scary. Get over it. Or get out of the way to let the next one through who has already made the decision to go for it Every Single Day. The choice is yours.

Wanna know the secret? You only have to make the decision once. You decide to do it Every Single Day and you no longer have to make the decision ever again. See how that worked out nicely like that?

Bonus Numbers Section for the Math Geeks

Let's say that 1 decision took just 1 minute. If we factored in not only time but unavailable brain power plus the stress on the system of "indecision" and stress, it is worth at least 3 minutes. Not to mention the positive effect that having already made that decision has on your nervous system gaining the ease of clarity and certainty, I would go so far as to say that this decision (to have already made the decision!) would actually gain time lost. So could this mean that we are turning back time and that this process not only doesn't cost you time, but earns you time. Could it be that we gain time? Are we making time? Are we creating more time than exists?

I told you it was for Math Geeks. Maybe it's for Existential Math Geeks--they have a different Facebook Group.

- Possible: twice every other day
- Impossible: yesterday
- Repossible: every single day

20

YOU CAN RUN, BUT YOU CAN'T HIDE.

You have to take risks. We will only understand the miracle of life fully when we allow the unexpected to happen.

— PAULO COELHO

You know the old saying, but it digs deep when you learn what you're truly hiding from.

You can run, but you can't hide from:

- Your dreams,
- Your passion,
- Yourself.

Just to play fair, here are things you can easily run and hide from:

- What others want (and/or expect) from you,
- Peer pressure,
- Sticking to a diet (or a plan or regimen etc.),
- Most everything else.

You can run. You can hide. But you can't run and hide.

Everything else you can outrun or outlast or outfox or out-something. But you can't outrun yourself. You can't hide from who you truly are. The solution? Let's cut to the chase:

Give In.

Stop all the running and hiding. Stop playing games. The torture, the torment, the challenges, the decisions, the back and forth. Give in (but don't give up) and allow, even if just for a second, that real dream to seep through.

It may be that you are the only one who knows what this is. That you're the only one who knows it exists within you. In fact, it's quite probable. On the one hand, that makes things a little easier because if no one is expecting anything from you because they don't know about it, you'd think that it would make it easier to hide.

But it's like putting masking tape over the oil light in the car. You're just applying a Band-Aid solution. You're hiding from the real issue, you're masking over the deeper drive at hand.

So give in, live a little. You don't have to tell anyone what you're doing (at least not yet). Just that you know that you've opened the can of worms, that you've cracked open the dam to just let a trickle through. Just a smidgen. It will be scary, relieving, and magnificent all at the same time.

- Possible: masking tape over oil light
- Impossible: masking tape fixes oil problem
- Repossible: change the oil

PART IV

PERSEVERANCE

21

INTRODUCTION

I do not think that there is any other quality so essential to success of any kind as the quality of perseverance. It overcomes almost everything, even nature.

— JOHN D. ROCKEFELLER

If you thought Part 3: Passion was difficult, Part 4 is going to hurt. On the other hand, if Part 3 was extremely painful, you're probably not even reading this as you've given up on your dream, moved to a country house in Vermont, and this page is being used as kindling for your roaring fire.

However, if Part 3 was easy for you, Part 4 is going to be even easier.

If you've come this far in this book, you already realize that **Passion provides energy. It's a source of energy, not a consumer of it.** If you have found a Passion or at least something that provides energy, then Perseverance is just keeping it going.

Whereas Passion may have gotten you started on running the marathon, even helped you register and put the number bib on with those tiny safety pins, Perseverance is what's going to get you to the finish line.

Part 5: Patience, just as a teaser, is what's going to take you over the finish line. Part 6: Play is the after party. (We're not invited just yet, sorry.)

Perseverance can mean that you go longer than you think necessary, longer than you want to, longer than you think possible.

Perseverance is the important step when you go beyond what you even thought imaginable back in the Passion stage.

Scary, I know.

But if you're OK with things like the unknown and the future and your Passion is clear, the Perseverance often means you're a kid in the candy store and the owner just whispered in your ear that you can stay as long as you want.

- Possible: turn around
- Impossible: finish without starting
- Repossible: chew an energy bar and get on with it

22

IF YOU COULD PRACTICE MORE, WOULD YOU?

In theory there is no difference between theory and practice. In practice there is.

— YOGI BERRA

Do you want to get better?

If you could practice all the time, would you? If you're doing what you love, do you even bother to call it practice?

Do you want to get better than the next guy or do you want to get better? Or both?

What's the joke about how fast do you need to go to outrun a bear? Faster than your friend.

Is it a competition? I don't know, is it? Is it for you? Do you want to be better because you enjoy doing it or do you want to be better for an "external" reason (e.g. praise, money, fame, competition)?

Does practice really make perfect? Do you care? What's perfect anyway?

What are you shooting for? Perfection? Good luck with that. Perfection is overrated. Perfection is some imaginary destination and we all know that the destination is overrated and the journey is the destination.

You know that, right?

Go ahead and practice. See what happens.

- Possible: practice
- Impossible: perfect
- Repossible: perseverance

23

TODAY IS A WHOLE LOT EASIER TO SEE AS YESTERDAY THAN AS TOMORROW.

The best preparation for tomorrow is doing your best today.

— H. JACKSON BROWN, JR.

I t's today. It's up to you what you call it.

Here's one of those nasty things that is simple but not easy. You have three elements: yesterday, today, and tomorrow. Each powerful in its own way.

Quick refresher class on time:

> *Yesterday: This is what you call what came before today. It's over, done, finished.*

> *Today: Now. Not before, not after. TIP: the only one you can do something with.*

> *Tomorrow: Not quite here yet, what comes later than now. You can't actually do anything with it. Yet.*

Simple words. You use them every single day. Yesterday. Today. Tomorrow. Let's ask some simple questions (careful, some of you might be offended):

- What did you do yesterday?
- Who are you today?
- Are your plans for tomorrow different from the plans for today? Different from yesterday?

Which questions make you smile? Which ones make you cringe? Which one made you want to stop reading?

It's a potentially vicious circle. If you didn't do yesterday what you then said you would do (back when you called it today) now it's today and there is no longer an opportunity to do what you wanted to do yesterday. It's over, it's done, there is no turning back the clock. No, really.

Aha, but you have tomorrow. In your back pocket. Your secret weapon. It's always there, isn't it? Always at the ready as the backup plan. Awesome. I have it in my back pocket too.

Spoiler Alert: this is where it gets nasty. You might want to avert your eyes.

Where does that leave us? Oh yes, not yesterday, been there. Not quite tomorrow, although we're both anticipating it with boundless energy and possibly even passion. That's when the Procrastination Workshop starts. But that's not it either. I'm going to spill the beans: all that's left is today.

It's the only one of the three that you can work with. It's the only one that you have control over.

Yesterday is too late. Tomorrow will never be here. No, honestly, by definition tomorrow never comes. There is only today. Do you see the choice?

Do you see that there actually is no choice?

There is today, now, the present moment, this moment that you're reading this. This is it.

It's up to you. What are you going to do with it?

- Possible: tomorrow
- Impossible: yesterday
- Repossible: today

24

BECAUSE "EVERY OTHER DAY PLUS WEEKENDS" IS TOO COMPLICATED.

We are what we repeatedly do. Excellence, then, is not an act, but a habit.

— ARISTOTLE

"Only brush the teeth you want to keep," says the dentist. Do you agree with the following statements?

- Only pursue your dream on days when you really feel inspired.
- Don't write when you know it's going to be crap--wait for inspiration to strike.
- Only work out when it feels good.

Consistency breeds creativity.

If you keep at it, the good stuff will come. You won't write a masterpiece every day. You might not lose a pound this week, but you're working on it.

Bite-size change that you create Every Single Day is truckloads more powerful than anything you might dream up every other Thursday evening.

> *"This whole Every Single Day thing, isn't it a little much? I mean, really, every single one? C'mon, give a guy a break!"*

If you've read this far, you might be onto something. This isn't for the faint of heart--this is for the heart.

Every Single Day isn't for something you have to do, it's for something you want to do.

But in fact, you want to do it so much that you have to do it. You have to because you can't not do it. It's a part of you and if you don't do it then you're not who you are--or at least who you know yourself to be. Until you want to be Every Single Day then you are not every single day and if you're not it every day then when are you it? On Tuesdays? Thursdays? What about weekends?

Get over the complexity and be who you are Every Single Day. We're not talking about losing 10 pounds, we're talking about becoming a healthy body. We're not talking about writing a book, we're talking about being an author. We're not talking about talking about someone you're not, we're talking about living, breathing, and being that person who you are.

When given the choice, it's really Every Single Day or never. I'm not forcing your hand, you're not forcing your hand. Only you know who you are; and what you need to do which will evolve into what you want to do to then what you can't not do to who you are.

Simple, right? Every Single Day.

Questions from the Front Lines

In case these same questions were rolling around in your mind, here are some answers.

> *"Every Single Day is too much. Can't I create a habit working less frequently?"*

Did you mean odd days or even days? What happens when it's the 31st and then the 1st, do I still have to do it? If you're using the words "too much" and "working" then you're in the wrong seminar. We're not talking about short-term change, we're talking about long-term transformation.

"My Sundays are for me."

Who, exactly are you doing this for, anyway, if not you? If you're doing it for someone else, then it's not going to be a long-term change no matter what you're doing. It's a chore and you're going to find a way out. We're looking for a way in.

> *"Can I skip a day if I'm on a deserted island and in bed with Dengue fever?"*

You can do whatever you want. You're not doing this for me, you're doing this for you. I don't care if you miss a day, I care if *you* care that you miss a day.

ESD Police Force

There is no "ESD Police." Well, not yet.

There is no eye in the sky who will see that you missed a day, that you truly were on that desert island with Dengue Fever. Oh, you'd like some ESD Police? Here's the police: tell people what you're doing. Make it public. Even if you start small and only tell a handful of people. Let others know that you're on a path towards change.

They'll get a kick out of it. At some point, you'll kick them out of it.

- Possible: every other day
- Impossible: Thursday evenings of months that end in "-ember"
- Repossible: Every Single Day

25

YOU'LL NEVER AGAIN SAY, "OH WELL. ANOTHER DAY WHERE I DIDN'T GET IT DONE."

Hope is the belief we might get it done, and faith is the knowledge we will get it done.

— TOM SHADYAC

Because you do it every day. No, sorry, Every Single Day. Have you ever had days where, at the end of the day, you say to yourself something like, "Dang it, I again didn't get it done. I'll do it tomorrow." There are variations on the theme:

- Ugh, I didn't manage to get started today.
- Oops, I missed a day. I'll catch up tomorrow.
- Sundays don't really count. Do they?
- I truly wanted to start tomorrow. I'll absolutely do it tomorrow.

When you have had the Every Single Day device surgically implanted in your skull, you'll never have to worry about saying things like that ever again. In fact, the device triggers dopamine production in the brain and you tend to smile ever so slightly when you hear phrases like this from other people. We've been working on a fix for that particular side effect, but on the other hand, we've had feedback that ... people kinda like it.

You see, when you get the ESD implant, you get it done. You don't have those regrets at the end of the day. You don't have them in the morning either, like a hangover, when you're pretty sure you didn't get it done the day before. Because you did get it done the day before. Because you'll get it done today. Because that's who you've become.

The implant changes your physiology. It truly, actually, and physically changes your body, how your mind works and, depending on what you believe you're made up of, it can change who you are. Crazy, I know.

Imagine. A person who gets it done. The woman who is the one people count on because she'll get it finished. In fact, you don't even have to ask her to double check, you just know because she's the one you can count on. Imagine that this person could be you. Then imagine that person is you. Then stop imagining and get it done.

We do need beta testers for the project. It doesn't hurt. Well, it doesn't hurt much. It depends on your perspective on pain. It might actually hurt a lot. But it might change who you are. Is it worth it? That's what we're going to find out.

What if you were the person who said things like this:

- Of course I got it done today.
- Oh, I don't need an extra day. It's finished.
- By the time the day is over, it will be started.
- You can count on me. I'm the kind of person who gets it done. Without asking. No reminders. Every Single Day.

If you already say these kinds of things, please sign up for our Masters of Time, Space, and Dimension Workshop.

If you're not quite there yet, but are still skeptical because, ahem, you can't really decide on it until tomorrow, sign up to get the release date and we'll let you know when you can start becoming the person you know you are.

HINT: the answer will always be "Tomorrow."

- Possible: We'll Get to it Tomorrow (Advanced Procrastination)
- Impossible: It Started Yesterday Workshop
- Repossible: Masters of Time, Space, and Dimension Workshop

26

THE "HOW" NO LONGER MATTERS.

Knowledge is of no value unless you put it into practice.

— ANTON CHEKHOV

To experience the highest levels of meditation, it doesn't matter what chair you're sitting in.

It's OK if the chair isn't your favorite, if your headphones only work through one ear, and you only have half an hour before you have to wake up the kids.

ESD for Biology

To learn biology, you don't need to sit at the table and take notes with a pen and paper. It's perfectly acceptable--even enviable--to walk through the woods and learn the chart of arthropods while watching your dog search for frogs.

To get better at basketball, the rim doesn't need a net, the ball can have a bulge in it, and you can wear your flip-flops.

When you practice Every Single Day, "how it's done" no longer matters. It only matters that you're doing the work.

Let me be the first to say that this does not mean that "going through the motions" is the same as "giving it all you've got." There's a scale, a spectrum, and, usually, the only person who is going to know if you're "cheating" is you.

On the other hand, after you become a gold-star rated ESDer, you have to give less and less effort to get to that same level of performance. Through your daily practice, be it in meditation, basketball, or biology, your brain has a grasp on the basics and you don't need to learn those every time. You advance as you go along and have to do less and less work to get to higher and higher levels.

Study Biology While Walking in the Woods

My son is 13. Enough said about the harsh laboratory testing conditions.

He thinks that studying means that we have to sit at his desk and "work hard." Good boy! But after a certain amount of time, you're allowed (encouraged even) to change the scenery, to rock the boat, the stir things up.

After you build a foundation for your practice, it actually helps to change things up. Your brain knows that you're going to be studying biology and can handle the change. In fact, it becomes so good at learning that you no longer have to try so hard. You can walk at the same time, throw a stick to the dog, and still remember that an example of an arachnid is a spider.

If we take something like meditation or writing, it's extremely fun to make sure that Everything is Perfect before you begin. But let's be honest here: we're really just looking for excuses to get started.

"Oh, I don't have the right pencil to take notes for my book. Can't start! Oh well!"

You know--and only you know--when you're making excuses and when you're ready to go.

The scene, the surroundings, the atmosphere matter less and less as you practice the Every Single Day method. It's about doing the work, about getting to the basics of what you're striving towards and everything else will fall away.

- Learn biology for your exam.
- Meditate to a higher level.
- Improve your basketball shot.

Force things for a while until they become habit. Once it kicks in (and you'll just know), then you play with the variables. But get first to the core, get it down pat.

Oh, and do it Every Single Day.

- Possible: study in your chair
- Impossible: wait for lightning to strike
- Repossible: learn at all costs under any circumstances

27

PRACTICE IS PERFECT

Practice is everything. This is often misquoted as Practice makes Perfect.

— PERIANDER

I f you're waiting around for perfection, take a seat and brew some tea. It's going to be a while.

"Practice, practice, practice. Oh when oh when am I going to get there?"

This squarely falls into the "Simple But Not Easy" category, but it's a mindset shift, a slight change of the angle of perception. It's still doing the same thing, but seeing it in a different light.

Practice Doesn't Make Perfect. Practice is Perfect.

Let's take my dear friend the marathon runner. One might think, well, he might even think, that the marathon, or worse yet, some certain time goal for completing that marathon, is his goal--or his perfect.

I'm just going to blurt it out in hopes it might sink in through blunt simplicity: his practice is his perfection.

When he is practicing, when he is running, he is perfect. He not only has already achieved his goal, he repeatedly achieves his goal. How often? Do you really have to ask? Every Single Day.

This is even crazier, but he might even achieve his perfect when he reaches that completion time. But then what? Has he reached perfection? Yay! Oh, but now what?

Yeah, exactly. Now what?

Could it be that reaching perfection could even be a "bad" thing? Marathon guy might then do what? He could either:

- Keep going and strive for better finish times.
- Be satisfied with his achievement and stay level.
- Relish in the accomplishment and slow down or quit altogether (as he achieved his goal, so he's done and can move on).

What if his Practice were his Perfect?

What if, Every Single Day, he achieved his goal? What if it weren't necessarily the goal in the most commonly used sense of the word, but it was just a habit or running was just a part of who he had become? What if running were the goal? Running became just a part of what he does, who he is, and now he can build on top of that and become more because he is achieving his goal all of the time and it's taking little or no effort or decision-making power or striving or trying?

He is building a solid foundation from which he can further excel. But we're not talking about speed or strength or even health or benefits.

When has he reached perfection?

When perfection is no longer his goal.

The practice is his perfection. He has risen above the "end goal" and is to a point where it is not a question of whether or not he achieves some time or some physical shape or something that occurs now and again.

The secret, if you've dared to read this chapter, is that he will then achieve those goals, the time, the health, the whatever it is that he wanted, but they are just icing on the cake and, sure, he enjoys them, but his perfection is his practice. His wins and successes are par for the course, they are just side effects of his consistent perfection.

- Possible: practice
- Impossible: perfection without practice
- Repossible: practice is perfect

28

LEARNING IS CUMULATIVE

Excellence is an art won by training and habituation. We do not act rightly because we have virtue or excellence, but we rather have those because we have acted rightly. We are what we repeatedly do. Excellence, then, is not an act but a habit.

— ARISTOTLE

We are what we repeatedly do.

Like training for a marathon, you don't start training the day before. You build on what you've already done.

Every day you're better. Even when you think you have a "bad day" you still have a day that is a step further along than the day before and a step closer to where you're heading.

You don't just start First Grade without having completed Kindergarten. Your learning is based on what you learned before and everything new is based on the foundation you have been building on. You can't just learn step 5 before getting through steps 1 through 4.

Here's the secret. Even on a bad day, even when you think you're not making any progress, even when you think you might even be regressing, you're moving forward. Through mistakes, you learn. With failure, you learn what success means. Through Every Single Day you're learning, improving, and moving forward.

Here's an even bigger secret. As you practice, as you learn, at some point the "basics" of what you're doing become automatic. **You no longer have to think about what you used to have to spend energy and thought on because your brain has learned it and you now do it automatically.**

This can be hard to grasp when you're starting out because it just seems too difficult.

Let's take skiing. At first, you can barely stand. You fall over just steps away from the ski rental office. But each day you learn a new skill and you no longer have to think about the very first basics. Soon you're learning more advanced techniques and your brain is freed up to learn those because it's no longer busy with the basics.

The basics become built in, a part of you, automated.

Because you no longer have to think about the basics, you can now focus on moving higher, getting better, and, here's the best part: you reach a level where you seek even higher goals, goals that you couldn't imagine back when you started.

The hard part is that you need to train your brain on the basics. You can't just skip ahead. It needs to learn it, it needs to be ingrained and become automatic and then and only then can you progress.

When you're starting out, this part is hard to believe but at some point, you are seeking goals and limits that you didn't even know existed back when you started.

Passion only gets you so far. Perseverance will get you to levels never before understood. In the next section, Patience, we'll go where you have never even imagined.

- Possible: practice
- Impossible: progress
- Repossible: practice and progress

29

THE $23,135 RECURRING PASSIVE INCOME POST

I write one page of masterpiece to ninety-one pages of sh*t. I try to put the sh*t in the wastebasket.

— ERNEST HEMINGWAY

I wrote one post and it has earned me over $20,000.

This is what I usually hear when I tell the story of my gold-mine post:

- "The post must have been epic!"
- "You must have worked on it for months!"
- "You certainly tricked out the SEO and bought ads to promote it!"
- "At least you expected it to be so popular!"
- "It must have been a really sexy and hot topic!"

Sorry, none of the above is what happened. Here's the big reveal:

One of my hundreds of posts hit the jackpot.

Over a course of several years, I wrote (usually really boring) posts about marketing topics and technical how-to stuff. I wrote lots of them. This was even before I was bitten by the ESD bug. Back then, I was on the Every Other Monday Except Holidays (EOMEH) schedule.

I wrote them to help my clients with marketing and technical mumbo jumbo. I also didn't really want to walk through the fix with each client on the phone separately so I wrote them up and posted them on my site.

Hundreds of the posts got little traffic. Some got more. A few hit it big. One, just one, made all that cash.

How did I know that this particular post was going to be the big winner?

I didn't.

Why didn't I just write the posts that would be big winners?

I'm not that clever.

Why didn't I skip the other 99 posts and write the 1 that hit the big time?

I needed to write the total of 100 because I didn't know which one was the good one.

Do you see where this is going? You can't just run the marathon. You have to train for it. You don't know which of your products is going to sell, so you test them, try them out, put them up for sale.

But they need to be out there. You can't hide this all in your mind and magically, one day it will be revealed which one is the golden egg.

- You run Every Single Day to stay in shape.
- You write Every Single Day because it feeds your imagination.
- You meditate Every Single Day because it lifts your soul.
- You _____ Every Single Day because it _____
  .

Hemingway couldn't just choose to write one page of masterpiece. He had to write the ninety-one pages first to then sift through it and find the one good one.

If you keep at it, you can turn the ratio in your favor and at some point, maybe you only have to write ninety pages, then eighty-nine ...

- Possible: wait for perfection
- Impossible: win every time
- Repossible: let it all out

30

OH BABY, IT'S COLD OUTSIDE. (AKA: NO ONE WILL NOTICE IF WE DON'T DO THIS.)

I've known entrepreneurs who were not great salespeople, or didn't know how to code, or were not particularly charismatic leaders. But I don't know of any entrepreneurs who have achieved any level of success without persistence and determination.

— HARVEY MACKAY

There are so many reasons (aka excuses) we shouldn't do this.

But we have done, we do, we will do.

My son and I wanted to practice some basketball. Let's do a quick roll call, see who else is in attendance:

1. It's really cold outside.
2. No one else is out here (see point #1).
3. No one is forcing us to go outside.
4. No one will notice if we do it--or if we don't.
5. It's below freezing. That means water turns to ice, fingers turn into sticks, and there aren't even puddles, but little frozen ice rinks for ants (refer to #1).

6. It might not help us improve.
7. Maybe we'll break a finger (see #5).
8. We want to get better and we're curious to know how to get there.
9. It's warmer inside.
10. They have hot fries in the deep fryer at Kwalitaria. Calling out our names, waiting on us, patiently. Did we mention they were hot?
11. Something larger than us is pulling us outside to practice.
12. It's not as accurate to shoot with gloves on.
13. I think the basketball is frozen and will explode.

That settles it. Let's see, it's about 11-2 in favor of the let's-just-stay-inside-and-say-that-we-went-out.

Which are the 2? Can you find them? Maybe it's only 1. Maybe 1 will beat out the other 12. Maybe 1 student will beat out the other 12. Maybe 1 team will win over the rest of the 12 other teams. One book will rocket to the top. One artist will rise above the others. One person just wants it more.

Because you can't stop learning, won't stop soaking it up, can only get stronger, smarter, better, faster and have more and more fun doing it.

Maybe you have a #14 that drives you. Maybe your own #14 is stronger than the other 13 and the next 13 to come. Do you recognize it? Can you put your finger on it? It's OK if you can't, it's perfectly fine if you can't put a label on it--labels are overrated anyway. It's a knowing that ranks higher than any doing or trying or even being.

What's your one thing that's keeping you moving? Keeping you not only in the game, but maybe even on top of your game?

For me, it's a combination of #11 with a heaping dose of #8. For my son, who wanted to go out in the first place, I think it's #11, then #8, but they could all just go down in flames because #10 is right in front of him.

- Possible: try
- Impossible: hope
- Repossible: know

PART V

PATIENCE

Don't worry, this section isn't so long.
   Just making sure you still have your sense of humor.

31

INTRODUCTION

Beware the fury of a patient man.

— JOHN DRYDEN

I f Perseverance was torture, this is just salt in the wound. Or wounds. Yeah, sorry.

But if Perseverance was like the time when you were on a long bike ride and at some point you no longer realized you were still pedaling, then this is going to be fun.

You see, dear reader, you have done the hard part--or at least what you thought was the hard part before you started. The "hard part" before you joined the ESD cult, I mean, team, was stuff like:

- taking the first step,
- hard work,
- blood, sweat, and tears,
- suffering,
- waiting (usually while suffering, maybe bleeding),
- long hours,
- torturous labor,

- etc.

You get the idea. Hard stuff. Not fun stuff. If that's what the Perseverance section was for you, I'm terribly sorry, but someone had to do it. Well, we all have to do it.

Well, sort of.

For most of us, we get stuck in Part 4: Perseverance. We grind it out, we work hard, we sweat, we bleed, we cry, we panic, we no longer care and then ... we give up. That's where Part 5 comes in: Patience.

I see the Patience section as something of a sly, aloof, but secretly brilliant sports coach. The coach is going to wait until you've exerted all of your energy, you've given it your absolute best, and you can't give any more. You want to give up. He truly wouldn't really care if you give up. You're just about to give up. In fact, you might be walking towards the coach on the other side of the gym floor to give up, to say you quit, to tell him it's just too much for you and you can't handle it because you don't know what to do anymore, you can't work any harder, you don't have any more sweat to spare, you are at the end of anything and everything you know how to do.

Then you're ready for Patience.

It's as if the coach wanted to make sure you really, truly, purely, and absolutely wanted it. The coach wants to see that you're ready to sacrifice, give up, and give in: surrender. You've gone beyond what you thought was possible, further than you thought you ever could. You've been patient, you've been good, no, you've been great. You've had your ups and downs but you're still here. You just don't know what to do anymore. You need to take it to the next level. Move up or move out.

It's time to move up.

Patience isn't about waiting for the coach to say you're awesome. Patience isn't about doing the same thing over and over and hoping that something will change. Patience is about that walk over to the other side of the court and knowing the coach might say you're cut and he might say you made the team. Patience is being ready for either answer.

The answer might be just on the other side of the wall you've been banging your head against. It's knowing that Part 6: Play is right on the other side. Patience might be finding a new door, tunneling under, or climbing over. It's about being open to the possibility that this all might not work out--but keeping going.

Patience is knowing that you're at the end of your rope, your abilities, and your ... patience. Understanding that you're not going to get there in a way that you know or recognize or understand. Patience is being open to a new path.

If Perseverance is peddling uphill, Patience is that first part on the mountain where the incline is less steep and you sense that the flat summit is just around the next bend. Part 6: Play is just around the next bend overlooking the downhill and the valley beyond. But first we need to get to the top. We need to rise up to conquer Patience.

- Possible: impatience
- Impossible: wait for change
- Repossible: patience

32

MEDITATION IS A SINGLE LETTER AWAY FROM MEDICATION ... AND MEDIATION.

Half an hour's meditation each day is essential, except when you are busy. Then a full hour is needed.

— Saint Francis de Sales (?)

W hat if the doctor scribbled the prescription and instead of "medication" wrote "meditation"?

I'm just going to bust right through the wall of Part 5: Patience and slip in what I consider the greatest tool that has propelled me further than any other tool--and all other tools combined.

Sure, hard work is necessary. Yup, you absolutely need that Passion to get you started. Perseverance will get you down the path and Patience will help you get to, well, to this. But frankly, we're still on the same horizontal plane. It might be at the top of the mountain, but we want to take it up a notch: fly or zoom downhill.

I'm positive there are glowing definitions and descriptions of meditation from people of all walks of life. Famous people, smart people, gurus, weirdos, western, eastern, northern, and southern.

Please, go learn about meditation and give it a try. Explore and discover on your own with my only request that you give it a go.

> -- *mediate: to bring about (an agreement, accord, truce, peace, etc.) as an intermediary between parties by compromise, reconciliation, removal of misunderstanding*

Meditation is also one letter more than "mediate."

Meditation is somehow the "mediator" between the heart and the mind and the unknown. It distills your hodgepodge of thoughts into a shimmering pot of clarity.

Have you ever stood in a lake where the water is so clear that you can see your feet? If you rustle up the sand with your toes and feet and there is sand everywhere, that's about how I see our everyday minds churning along. What meditation is for me is when you don't move for a few minutes and all of that sand settles back down and it's clear again.

For some of you reading this book who have been, hopefully, happy so far with how I've arranged things to help you get from A to B or C, you might think that this chapter is going off the deep end, into La La Land, into fairy dust and Tinkerbell.

If where I am now is the Deep End, if this is La La Land and there's some fairy dust and I might get to meet Tinkerbell? I. Am. All. In.

I honestly feel that I cannot do meditation justice as a chapter of this book. It merits its own section, its own book, its own series. But on the other hand, it's as simple as the Every Single Day philosophy. **It's both simple and easy ... or at least it's easy once you realize that it's simple and you stop trying to make it complicated.**

If you were hoping for at least a few practical tips from me with my experience with meditation, here are a handful.

Meditation is ... what takes you up and over the wall when you were pretty sure that you were just going to sit down in front of it and give up ...

the clarity of an idea that comes up and through a muddy pond of other ideas so perfectly and purely that you at least have to give it a try ... the imagination of what Charlie Holiday might do next in a story ... it's innocence, purity, clarity, gratefulness, happiness and then all of those ... the energy source that powers me through Every Single Day ... what gives me the confidence and clarity to know which path to take ... the strength to power on ... the answers to know which way ... the silence to hear ...

I'm sure I'm not describing it well. For something so dear and near to my heart, for something so important in my life, I don't have the words to begin to describe what it has done for me. I hope it can at least give you a taste of the power it harnesses ... but of course, that power is you.

Remember when you were a kid and you first learned how to ride a bike? What if I told you how the gears worked and the brakes and the history of the rubber tire? First of all, being a kid, you wouldn't have cared.

Then I brought you through a hands-on workshop where we built bicycles from scratch and welded the parts together. You might find the welding part kind of cool, but it wouldn't have helped you ride the bike.

The best way to learn to ride a bike is to jump on and give it a go. Maybe first try it on some grass, somewhere that falling is going to be less painful--because you're guaranteed to fall.

If you want to stop falling, you'll soon figure out that you need to pedal, steer, and balance at the same time. Meditation is much the same. You just have to try it for yourself and it will be worth several weekend workshops and a handful of books.

Talk to someone who's done it. Maybe even try it together with a friend who's a fan of meditation. But if there's one thing that I can recommend to get to the next level, this is it. By a long shot.

- Possible: meditate tomorrow
- Impossible: meditate yesterday
- Repossible: meditate today

For an inspirational video about many "famous" people who meditate: https://goo.gl/nkg7tf

On a meta note, I decided to put this chapter in Part 5: Patience as a tool to get to Part 6: Play. I'm not 100% sure, but at least in my experience, I wouldn't have been able to reach the level of Part 6: Play without meditation.

33

THIS IS HOW YOU LIVE TO BE 103 YEARS OLD.

Creativity is a habit, and the best creativity is the result of good work habits.

— TWYLA THARP

Creativity in, creativity out.

Life needs circulation. Even a car's engine needs to turn, sometimes to turn fast and clean out the gunk that builds up over time. But there's a process, a flow, a circle, a cycle.

We have so much input every day: media, conversations, thoughts, even just taking a walk. It's practically a hurricane of overwhelming sensory data. What's a brain to do with it all?

We need an outlet.

All of this information is coming in. Think of a garden hose in a bucket--but it never turns off. It just keeps filling, keeps coming in. Pretty quickly, it's going to overflow. Is that then "wasted" water? What if we could use it, harness it, filter it and then send it back out as something even more useful?

This is how creativity works.

We need input to have output. We talk about The Blank Page and we are going to fill it with words, paint, or a business plan, but we have to have something to work with, something that fills our brains that will fill that page (or canvas or sound waves or ?). Is the input just anything that we take in? Is a walk in the park the same for Person A as it is for Person B?

If Person A walks in the park and doesn't take anything in, maybe they need less to offload. Maybe there is less circulation of thoughts, ideas, and creativity. If Person B walks through the park and takes it in, filters what they want, repels what they don't want, sees things maybe others wouldn't see and then has an outlet, then it builds a circle, a cycle of thoughts and ideas that are filtered through Person B's mind to become something else, something new, something different.

My dear neighbor Tony recently turned 103 years old. How many people over, say, 80 do you know who live like this:

1. He lives on his own. No help, no nurse, nobody else. My mom goes by occasionally.
2. He is in excellent health. In recent years, he's been using a walker, but he gets around fine--especially if it's to show you his art.
3. He works. Sorry, did you catch that? He works. I know, ahem, 13-year olds who are too lazy to work. That's 90 years younger. But he doesn't call it work, it's what he loves to do. This is creativity, this is output.
4. He has a sense of humor. I tend to classify older people into the glass half full and glass half empty. His cup runneth over.
5. He reads the newspaper, watches movies, and listens to music. He especially likes André Rieu. I bring him DVDs from Holland of Mr. Rieu. This is input.
6. He eats white bread, doesn't drink alcohol, and often has frozen TV dinners. (If you don't know what a TV dinner is, it's better that way.)
7. He gets at least 8 hours of sleep a night.

There are probably other reasons he's reached such a milestone in years. I'm focusing on #3 and #5.

Take a human body. Or a car engine. Take your pick. Both need to move, to turn, they survive (and thrive) on input and output. Stuff goes in and stuff goes out. The more it moves or turns or cycles, the better. It keeps it clean, healthy, and alive.

What are your inputs?

What are your outputs?

Are you keeping them running, in good shape, and well oiled? You think it might lead you to a longer, happier, more fulfilled life?

If you're only producing, maybe you're not taking in enough. Or maybe you're only taking it all in and you have no outlets. Part of Patience is finding that balance through experience, experimentation, and examination.

- Possible: getting older
- Impossible: getting younger
- Repossible: creating your art

34

WHAT IF YOU COULD FREE UP YOUR BRAIN TO PUT YOUR CREATIVITY INTO TURBO OVERDRIVE?

Creativity is just connecting things. When you ask creative people how they did something, they feel a little guilty because they didn't really do it, they just saw something. It seemed obvious to them after a while. That's because they were able to connect experiences they've had and synthesize new things.

— STEVE JOBS

If you are online, watch this video: https://goo.gl/V11kN8. It's four minutes.

If you're not online, it's a video of four people singing a song and performing a complex hand clapping routine that looks, frankly, like rocket science to me. I'm pretty sure I can't rub my belly and pat my head at the same time.

Do you think they're consciously thinking about what their hands are doing?

They are also probably not struggling to remember the lines of the song. Ideally, they're just having a good time and maybe their only conscious "decisions" are whom to look at, maybe to even think of something else, or about how two days ago when they were practicing, one of them fell off of her chair and they all had a good laugh.

Because they're not spending energy on the words or the notes or the timing or what their hands are doing, they have precious time to let go and relax. Which is why they seem relaxed.

Have you ever noticed that in a pro basketball game at the highest level, even when it's down to the wire and a make-or-break situation, they don't seem nervous? Even if they are somewhat nervous, they don't show it. They have been there so many times that what they are about to do is just ingrained in their minds so deeply that they don't have to think--in fact, they're going to perform better if they don't think.

Let's say you had to:

1. Fold laundry,
2. Write down your grocery list,
3. Work on the next chapter of your book (or something creative),
4. Walk the dog.

What if you could free up your brain to put your creativity into turbo overdrive?

What you'd really like to do is #3, the creative bit. But you know you have to get #1 done and #2 has to get done at some point in the day. #4 is pleasant and you can do that at any time (well, don't wait too long ...).

What if you did it in this order:

1. Write down your grocery list. It's now out of sight, out of mind--literally. It's off your plate and you don't have to think about it again. You don't even need to think about it at the grocery store because you have a list. This frees up a few cylinders in the engine of your mind.
2. Walk the dog. Get outside. Laundry can wait. Maybe put it on tumble dry ...

3. While walking the dog, you're going to Work on the next chapter of your book (or something creative). Hopefully, you've got the walking the dog thing to the point where you don't need to think about it. You leash him up, hopefully can let him loose in the park or woods and you don't have to do anything or think about it anymore. Hey, he's not worried about you, don't worry about him. No, you don't have pen and paper. No, you don't have your laptop. Good -- they are distractions anyway. What is the outcome of the next chapter? What does the character feel at the end of the chapter? How are the actions going to take place to get him there? Your dog is fine. Keep working on your chapter.

4. When you're back home and you've written out the mental notes you took on your walk, you can fold laundry. You do this automatically, you don't have to debate whether to fold in the right sleeve or the left sleeve first, it just happens. Allow yourself to work some more on your chapter. Go over your notes in your mind as you mindlessly fold laundry.

Folding laundry is how the musicians in the video see their clapping. They've done it so often, they've practiced so many times they don't need to think about it. In fact, maybe, while they're singing, while they're recording this song, what they might be thinking about is what might be even better for their next song.

Did you catch that? **While they're "busy" with what they used to find difficult, they're now able to do that unconsciously which frees up brainpower to think about how it might be better next time.**

Can you imagine having all of that available brain power at your disposal? If so much of what you did was automatic or subconscious that you had left over, extra mind capacity to think of the next big thing?

What can you work on to the point where you have it down pat?

You know it in your sleep, you don't have to think about it and in fact, thinking about it makes it worse? You don't think about walking your dog, driving your car, or riding your bike. What can you learn, practice and ingrain into your brain so that it becomes a habit? What if you even wanted to do it Every Single Day because you enjoyed it and understood the turbo boost that it would give you? That it becomes something that you just do?

Once you have it down, here's the most exciting part: **because you've been using so much of your brain for the basics, it didn't have the space to think of new ideas.** What if you stood on top of where you used to strive towards and started your creative process from there?

Where might you go? What might you achieve? Seemingly boundless, right?

Have fun with that.

How am I doing it?

By Writing Every Single Day, I have "demoted" the writing aspect to the point where it's just automatic, I just do it, it's just something I do. It's the basis, the foundation. When do I get creative? By triggering my writing mind by doing what I do Every Single Day, but knowing that it needs no additional help or concentration, my mind is wide open for what's coming, what's new, what's going to work and, even better, things I can't even imagine from that lower-level mind. Fun, right?

- Possible: just try harder
- Impossible: survive and create (at the same time)
- Repossible: delegate the basics (survival) to the subconscious and allow the conscious space to create

PART VI

PLAY

THIS IS GOING TO BE FUN.

35

INTRODUCTION

Strong emotions such as passion and bliss are indications that you're connected to Spirit, or 'inspired,' if you will. When you're inspired, you activate dormant forces, and the abundance you seek in any form comes streaming into your life.

— WAYNE DYER

If you've skipped ahead to read the end of this book, I'm afraid it's going to either be anti-climactic, boring, or both.

Do you know what it feels like to reach the top of Mount Everest, raise up your arms in jubilation, and breathe in the sweet air of victory?

Yeah, no, neither do I. Because I haven't climbed Mount Everest. I haven't even seen the mountain. I'm not even sure what country it's in. I haven't spent the grueling hours and days and nights slogging up the rocky cliffs, risking life and limb, and taking selfies of my fatigued self in order to reach the summit.

I haven't put in the work so I can't taste the sweet victory. Even if I were helicoptered to the top, I couldn't experience the feeling of climbing to the summit. In a word, I hadn't earned it.

"Play" would have meant nothing to me a few short years ago. Sure, I recognize the word: kids do it at the playground, I watch people play sports, but there's a meaning of play that's only come to me recently.

"But I was kinda shooting for riches, fame, and an award for my efforts!" I hear you cry out. This is better.

"So will I be able to levitate above water and see the world from a new perspective?" You're getting closer.

"Is it something I can't touch, can't quite put my finger on, but a power within me I previously only experienced perhaps as an innocent child or during moments of pure bliss and ecstasy?" We're getting there.

As I write this, adjectives and nouns are flying through my mind as I try to put my definition of Play into words. Perhaps if I just let them fly onto the page it will help get us there.

Play is ...

Play is ... confidence. It's not that I can do everything, but I can do anything. See the difference?

Play is ... a "knowing" that was previously, well, unknown.

Play is ... a certainty or at least the willingness to try anything or go anywhere because the path is clear. Clarity.

Play is ... joy. Joy is an overused word that shows up often on greeting cards, yet it's one of those feelings when you have it, you deeply appreciate it.

Play is ... lightness. Scientists could possibly prove me wrong, but it's as if my feet don't completely touch the ground anymore. But it's only partly in the feet. The more important part of Lightness is in my heart. Decisions are easier, problems are challenges or experiments, people are funnier. I'm hilarious. (I'm laughing out loud as I type these words.) That's Play in action. I'm laughing at myself, for myself, in spite of myself, and with myself.

Which brings me to Happy. If Joy is the deep waters of the ocean, Happy is splashing about in the kiddie pool. It's silly, shallow, and you lose track of time. Play is ... happy.

Play is ... timeless. I'm not in a hurry. I'm happy to be the Turtle. I'll get there. Because I'm enjoying the ride.

Remember the Tortoise and the Hare? I saw the hare, that speed demon who took off from the starting line so long ago. His rotting carcass was on the side of the road. That was awhile back. His head was turned back towards, well, me. He was so far ahead, yet I didn't care. I wasn't in the same race. In fact, I'm not in a race at all. It's not a competition, there's cooperation. I'm in the game. I am the game. I'm playing.

This is Play.

- Possible: work
- Impossible: try
- Repossible: play

36

LINEAR VS. EXPONENTIAL

I spent many years slogging away and getting nowhere. Then I spent some more years slogging away harder and getting somewhere. Then I spent less energy and less time and got beyond where I thought I could ever go: anywhere.

— Bradley Charbonneau

L et me explain. With math.

I'm a card-carrying math nerd. Well, I shouldn't say nerd. Maybe I'm a secret math superstar, a spy, a secret agent of math. I use its powers beyond what the mere third-grade substitute math teacher can grasp. If math is about as fun for you as pulling hair out of the shower drain, I'll give you a pass to skip this chapter.

Ah, I joke, but then, I do not. You can't skip this chapter.

For you math phobes out there:

- a linear line is a straight line.
- an exponential line is a curved line (but not just any curved line!)

That's about all you need to understand. The linear line is constant, predictable, and easy to calculate. It can go down, straight across, up, or straight up. The exponential line is curved, although the rate at which that curve changes also increases.

I'll save you the mathematical formulas. Let's use a simple financial example to explain. We'll start with $100.

If you put your $100 under your mattress, it will (hopefully) stay there and after a year, it will still be $100. Dare I say that many of us live our lives like this. Enough said.

Or you could invest your $100 at the bank where they give you "simple interest" and you earn, let's say 5% per year so that after one year, you have $105. However, this isn't compound interest, so the next year you also earn 5% or $5 and now you have $110. Can you see the straight line? It's increasing each year, but by a consistent factor.

If we jump over to compound interest, that $100 after one year is still only $105. However, the following year, the 5% is multiplied by the $105 and we'd get $110.25. While it seems small, the point with compound interest is that it's "growing on the growth." The rate at which it increases keeps getting bigger.

After ten years, here's what you'd have in the three scenarios:

1. $100 (mattress)
2. $150 (simple interest)
3. $162.89 (compound interest)

Enough with the numbers and the math. If you don't think those numbers are exciting, add some zeroes if you like if that makes you feel better. I'm not so interested in numbers at this point. I'm interested in the *rate of change* and the aspect of *compound learning* and progress.

We're compounding our knowledge to the point where we are learning on top of the learning. Every Single Day we add not only to what we knew the day before yesterday, but also to yesterday. It compounds. It multiplies. It grows exponentially.

There may be days when you think you're slogging away, that

things are progressing linearly. No worries. Then there will be days when you are rocketing out of the atmosphere at speeds you had previously not known were possible.

The best part, in my humble opinion, is when you think you're progressing linearly--or not at all--but you're just in front of a break-through. You might not know it. It seems you might be stuck, but, if you're a true, card-carrying ESD Soldier, you'll carry on and you keep going. You might be stuck in the mud, but you rev your engines and keep at it, you sway back and forth, trying to get unstuck, you give it one last push, one big pull, wanting to give up, then you're out. But you're more than out, you've leapfrogged the mud puddle and you shoot over to something beyond what you planned, even beyond the linear expectation of where you might have ended up. You might even be somewhere you're not familiar with, but it's exciting and fun and new.

That's exponential power.

Whereas the $162.89 might not excite you, if you think in terms of our progress, that's where it gets interesting.

Let's look at a case study. Any takers? Hmm. No hands up? OK, fine, oh there's one: me.

1. I didn't write at all.
2. I wrote every day. Non fiction, research-related stuff.
3. I dabbled in fiction. I exploded.

A few short years ago, I would not have said that I was heading towards writing fiction. I was a solid, down-to-earth nonfiction writer who was going to write manuals on, well, something or other.

I kept going. I got stuck. I moved along. I struggled. I succeeded. I failed. I slowed down. Charlie Holiday appeared in my life.

A character appeared in my imagination and I wrote down his story. It wasn't so much that I was creating his story, it's more than I was being told his story or more accurately, I was being shown his story on an IMAX-size theater in my mind. Then I wrote it down.

I wanted more, but it wasn't coming from my own creation, my own brain. I was just the messenger, I was just the transcriber. My fingers tapped and Charlie's story came to life. People asked me what was going to happen next and I would respond that I didn't know, but I also wanted to know. (Want to meet Charlie? https://goo.gl/VJcQVW)

That, in my world, is exponential, unexpected progress and I'm not sure I know of a curved line more beautiful.

- Possible: linear
- Impossible: divide by zero
- Repossible: exponential

37

BETTER TOGETHER

The real energy occurs in each connection between two people, which can bring about exponential returns.

— Tom Rath

D o any of these sound familiar?

- I got this.
- I don't need any help.
- I work better alone.
- Other people slow me down.
- Did I mention that I can do this all by myself?
- I'm really a solopreneur.
- I work more efficiently and effectively on my own.

I spent the better part of a decade, not so much unwilling to work with others, but simply not understanding the exponential possibilities working with others brings.

Remember the chapter called "Linear vs. Exponential"?

Better Together is even easier math. No multiplication! No exponents! Yippee! Here are the equations:

$1 + 0 < 1$

$1 + 1 > 2$

(The " < " symbol means less than. The " > " symbol means greater than.)

Both seem, according to the laws of mathematics, wrong. I agree. According to math, to the linear world, they are wrong.

But we want to expand beyond the straightforward, expected linear world and move into the more unknown world of Math That Doesn't Make Sense.

$1 + 0 < 1$

You + No One < You

$1 + 1 > 2$

You + Someone Else > Both of You

I have improved my math skills to realize that $1 + 1$ is no longer just 2, it's much more.

Let's get beyond the numbers.

One Plus One Equals: The Unknown

A partner brings in ideas you didn't, don't, and won't have. That's the beauty of looking outside yourself. You know what you get with yourself (same old, same old). With a partner, it opens up possibilities you didn't know existed. Maybe they're terrible, but maybe they're fresh and exciting. One thing is certain: they're not yours. (Hint: that's a good thing.)

A friend visited and we riffed ideas back and forth for hours. Nothing seemed to come of it until the next morning when it became clear what I needed to do the following year. I might have had thoughts around the topic, but because he was there and he thinks "bigger" and "broader" than I do, it rustled up my brain and got me thinking bigger and broader and we came up with an idea that was bigger than anything I had thought of on my own.

Cooking with Chemistry

Your known and their unknown mixed with a pinch of your unknown and a dollop of their known brews into a delicious stew of something you never could have cooked up yourself.

Accountability Partners

We all know you'll get it done, but an accountability partner is more than a watchdog. A partner brings you up to a higher level just because of the idea that someone else is working with you ... and might occasionally look over your shoulder.

One plus one is more than two. You plus someone else is greater than you. You plus someone else is greater than the someone else.

Build a team, find a partner, at least get a co-mentor. Work together, then work in parallel. Work on your own, then collaborate. Be your own mind, but be open to theirs. Get over yourself. Let it go. Be bigger than yourself. Be greater than two. Be Better Together.

- Possible: $1 + 0 < 1$
- Impossible: $1 + 0 = 2$
- Repossible: $1 + 1 > 2$

38

COAST

When you're that successful, things have a momentum, and at a certain point you can't really tell whether you have created the momentum or it's creating you.

— ANNIE LENNOX

W hen you do the work of peddling up the hill, you get to reap the benefits and coast.

Does it seem like you're still only pedaling uphill? Are you reading ahead here in Part 6: Play, but you're really stuck back in Part 4: Perseverance? Do you never get a break? Where is that summit anyway?

Or maybe everything is going your way, all of your dreams are falling into your lap like silent snowflakes. It's all coasting downhill and easy and magnificent.

If it's all uphill and you've been working (Perseverance) at for what seems like forever (Patience), take a side road off the mountain to catch your breath and regroup (Play). The downhill will re-energize you and let you rest and focus on which hill should be next. Even if you're not sure there's a flat stretch ahead, stop peddling so hard and take it easy. Or maybe there's a steep ascent you can find (work hard fast) with a long, slow downhill that will bring you slowly but surely to your goal (work soft slow).

If you're rolling even on the slightest of descents, let your legs rest and let the power of your momentum pull you forward. You've worked hard to get to this point, but you can't just go go go endlessly. Celebrate the smallest of wins, enjoy the wind in your hair and gear up for the next incline.

If you notice you're coasting, you can either enjoy the ride or take that extra momentum to explore a route you might not have otherwise taken. Coasting is confidence and you can ride it far.

Diving deeper into the cycling analogy, there are times when you're pretty certain you're riding on flat ground, then one of three things happens:

1. It feels like it's somewhat uphill,
2. It feels like it's just flat,
3. It feels like there's the slightest of downhill.

One secret to living ESD is when the reality is #2 but you feel like it's #3 and you're cruising, you're somehow coasting when it's actually flat and you shouldn't be able to do this. A certified ESD Master can turn #1 into #3.

Where are you at this point? Stuck in a low gear and struggling up the mountain? On the backside and flying so fast bugs are between your teeth? Found a leveled-out side road to catch your breath? Or maybe you've achieved some momentum and you're experiencing the beauty and power of that point where you're moving without much effort at all: The Coast.

- Possible: seek out the flats
- Impossible: uphill forever
- Repossible: coast

39

THE CRUISE SHIP & THE SAILBOAT

I'm not afraid of storms, for I'm learning how to sail my ship.

— Louisa May Alcott

Which is more powerful? Which uses more power? Which are you?

They are analogies as personality types or energy sources within us. We're either The Cruise Ship or The Sailboat. Let's have a quick look at both types.

The Cruise Ship

Massive. Power. Massive power. It can transport 5,000+ people and seems to glide through the roughest of seas. It's a floating fortress, a city on the water, it's magnificent.

The engine room is a churning, burning center of hot energy. It's constantly pushing out the force to propel the vessel forward, but it also has an insatiable need for more and more energy to burn. It's loud in the engine room, it's dirty, and everyone in there is wearing earplugs and is covered in soot. It's impressive, powerful and daunting.

Massive power forward, but it comes at a cost.

Turning is difficult and slow. In fact, stick to the course you're on and try not to diverge too much because it takes such effort to make a shift. That said, if you're powering forward, it's going to be difficult to stop you. We all just hope you're going the right way.

When things break down, there's not much to do other than try to fix all of the complicated parts that makes up the engines and the rotors and the propellers. You may occasionally run out of fuel. You can replenish the tanks, which can be draining, time consuming, or even prohibitively expensive (financially or otherwise). In order to prevent things from breaking down, you usually want to keep the ship afloat and churning at all costs.

The Sailboat

The sailboat glides through the water like a fish. More like it belongs in the water, moving almost with the water, as if it's going downstream, as if the entire ocean is streaming in the direction the sailboat is going.

Not only is the propulsion of this vessel through the water effortless, it could even gather more power. Because the force driving the motion is not your own, we could harness even more power through bigger sails, a better knowledge of sail positioning, or even water intake. Because this energy is coming from somewhere other than ourselves, we only need to guide it in the direction we want to go, make sure the sails are properly aligned to gather the most efficient and effective gusts of wind and sit back and decide where to go next.

Agile and natural, it can be more powerful than any engine.

If, however, there is little or no wind, you're not really going anywhere. There's that little outboard backup motor, but it's mostly for emergencies and putting around while you're waiting for the source energy (the wind) to pull you forward once again.

The wind picks up and all you need to do is guide the path

forward. Adjust the sails, the smaller ones, the larger ones, the ropes and pulleys. It's more like you're holding on and going with it, you're using power that is not yours, is larger than yourself, and you are just along for the ride.

It can become effortless once you get the handle of it and understand it--or at least accept that this is so. You can also try to fight it, to go against it and you might have some successes, but in the end, you will succumb. The wind wants to go the same direction as you're going, it wants to take you that way. You can also angle your direction to get the most use of the wind at its greatest strength. It's the way you're supposed to go anyway, so surrender and let it take you.

Do you resonate clearly with one or the other?

Back in Passion and Perseverance, you hopefully felt like the cruise ship: powerful, unstoppable, churning through the roughest of high seas.

Patience might teach you to abandon ship, change course, or row the dinghy to the sailboat in the distance. When you climb aboard, you feel it immediately. You feel the power of Play and what was pushing and churning is now pulling and sailing.

Welcome aboard.

- Possible: motor
- Impossible: row (upstream)
- Repossible: sail

YES, YOU CAN FORCE THE FLOW STATE.

When a story is flying along, and I'm so into it that my 'real' world goes away, it can feel magical. I cease to be, my desk and computer ceases to be, and I am my character in his world. Psychologists call this a 'flow state,' and it's better than publication, money, awards, fame.

— NANCY KRESS

"**B**ut I need a quiet space and my favorite coffee cup and my dog at my feet and only in the morning and ... "

I don't buy it.

Don't get me wrong. I used to believe it. But now that I know how to attain the flow state on a regular basis, I don't fall for anyone who says they can't achieve it.

Here's what Wikipedia says about Flow:

> *"In positive psychology, flow, also known as the zone, is the mental state of operation in which a person performing an activity is fully immersed in a feeling of energized focus, full involvement, and enjoyment in the process of*

the activity. In essence, flow is characterized by
complete absorption in what one does." -- Wikipedia

This is the good part, " ... complete absorption in what one does." That's what we're after, what many of us are seeking on a regular basis--or even once in awhile would be nice! That state of mind where time flies by (and stands still), where you don't think, you just do or act. It's when you aren't necessarily yourself, you might even see yourself as a sort of messenger as you are transferring or transmitting the message from a higher power.

If I lost you on that last bit, I'm not sure you've reached a flow state.

Remember Simple but not Easy? Yeah, that's what's going on here.

It is simple. It's a state. Once you know how to get there, then it's also easy. Tricky, right? Not so much.

In case you need a real-world example, here's what happens when I'm in the flow state when I'm writing.

It's like I'm watching a movie and writing down what I see. The crazy part is I'm not the director, or the producer, or even an actor in this movie. I wrote the first few chapters of a novel recently and I was as eager as the reader to learn what was going to happen next. Because I honestly didn't know. I kept "watching" (the movie in my imagination) and kept writing it out so I could get to what was going to happen next. It was thrilling, shocking, and yes, way, way, way fun!

In fact, I can't think of anything more fun than being in the flow state. Wow, dare I write this hidden in a late chapter in the final section of this book? Flow state is what we're aiming for. Flow state is like a drug-induced high, except the drug is you--when your passion turns into play and takes over your mind.

In my research, I've found we can achieve this state with practice, intention, repetition, patience, and, once you get there, a dollop of play.

All of the previous steps help you get to Flow State, but Play is what keeps you there.

"Dude, sounds awesome. I got the example. Tremendous. So please, do tell, how do you get into it voluntarily?"

It's simple. Practice.

I've got a bit of a thing for Every Single Day. I'm a card-carrying member of the ESD Society and I now know, from experience, that we can bring about the flow state quite easily. It's simple, it's easy.

1. Make it happen.
2. Do again whatever it was that you did in step 1.
3. Repeat.

Our minds are like muscles. We can work them out. We can train them. We can get them into shape. You can't just jump off the couch, turn off House of Cards and go run a marathon if you're not in running shape. But you can run around the block. That's Step 1.

If you work at it every day, no, sorry, Every Single Day, you build that muscle, you get into shape and you can fall into the flow state.

I'm going to stop trying to convince you and just let you have it. Give it, oh, I don't know, 10 Days. If you're a writer, here's a free 10-Day Writing Experiment to get you started [https://goo.gl/g89xhz].

When should you start? Oh, oh, I know! Let's see, uh, today is good.

Let me know how it goes.

- Possible: push
- Impossible: pull
- Repossible: flow

41

EXPECT THE UNEXPECTED

If you do not expect the unexpected you will not find it, for it is not to be reached by search or trail.

— HERACLITUS

This chapter could very well sum up the Part 6: Play section. After you've gone from linear to exponential, you've teamed up with partners, you've jumped the ship and are now the captain of your sailboat, and now you're cruising along in the flow state, this is what you can expect now. Expect the unexpected.

"But what's the roadmap? Where do I go? How do I, exactly, do this?" I hear you cry out.

"If you expect magic in every encounter, you find it."

— ADAM ROBINSON, US CHESS FEDERATION LIFE MASTER,
AND CO-FOUNDER OF THE PRINCETON REVIEW

It's a mindset shift, a priorities alteration, a tweak to your perspective.

You're now exponential, you're no longer going this alone, your sailboat is nimble, you're heading in the right direction powered by forces greater than your power (e.g. the wind) and it's time to begin to expect the unexpected.

Allow for surprises. Be open to good fortune. Make luck. Share power. Give more than you get. Create more than you consume. Believe in your own magic.

If you dig deep, go quiet, and know you don't have to tell anyone, not even me, you know you have magic within you. I won't quiz you, I won't ask you to prove it, or tell me what it is, but you have it and you know it.

Let that out of its cage. Expect what it can do, but it's unexpected, so just let it do its thing. What is its thing? Who knows. It might arrive tiny, it might bowl you over. It might be a tap on the shoulder, a comment someone makes, an unexpected gift, or a wink from a stranger. Just be ready for it, keep your eyes and ears open for it.

It may sound contradictory to "expect a surprise," kind of like pretending you don't know about the surprise party they're throwing for you, but, well, that's exactly it. You know it's coming, but you don't necessarily know how or what or when or who or why. But you know it's coming. That's expecting the unexpected.

- Possible: expect the expected
- Impossible: unexpect the expected
- Repossible: expect the unexpected

PART VII

PERORATION

Yeah, I had to look it up, too.

> *Peroration: a long speech characterized by lofty and often*
> *pompous language; the concluding part of a speech or*
> *discourse, in which the speaker or writer recapitulates*
> *the principal points and urges them with greater*
> *earnestness and force*

We might get a little "lofty" and we could shoot for a bit of "pompous language" while we're lofting about. While we're in dictionary mode: pompous: characterized by an ostentatious display of dignity or importance.

Sounds about right.

42

INTRODUCTION

I'd rather regret the things I've done than regret the things I haven't done.

— LUCILLE BALL

I've transformed my life and I'd like to help you transform yours--but only if you really, really, really want to.

There's just that "if" in there. But you've got that, right? We're in Part 7, if you don't have it yet, you still have a few chapters to reign it in. But seriously, if you're here reading Part 7, I'd venture to say that you do really, really, really want to.

I've been there, done that. I've been down in the dumps, crawled out of holes, soldiered on when it wasn't cool to do so. I've kept going, I tried to keep my head up. I thought, "What would my decision be if I saw this from the perspective of me as an 80-year old?" I tried to keep things in perspective. I counted and I'm pretty sure I only have one life to live. I don't really talk to too many cats, but word on the street is they have nine lives. Good for them. I'm going to do what I can with this one and when it's over, we'll see how that next one goes.

When there are requirements for something that I'd like to do, it's always encouraging to hear about people who did it and then compare to see if you "have what it takes" to do what they did. Let's see: become an NBA basketball player? Not really going to happen (of course, nor do I really want it to). Write the top-grossing best seller of all time? Yeah, sure, it'd be fun, but do I really, really, really want it? Nah. Live a life where Every Single Day I discover something new, see something bright and shiny, shoot love out of my heart, and follow the dream I've had most of my life? Yeah, that I really, really, really want.

What do you want? What do you really, really, really want?

What's between the you of the past and the you of today and the you of the future?

I hope that in this book I've given you the tools to at least take that first step, at least change your mindset, or know that it's possible. If today isn't Day One, then when is it? If it's next Tuesday, fine, but then get started next Tuesday.

But why wait? Why spend another day being the person you don't really want to be? Are you a cat? Let's get this party started in this life-time. When exactly?

Ooh, ooh! I know! I know!

Today.

- Possible: tomorrow
- Impossible: yesterday
- Repossible: today

43

ESD SIDE EFFECTS

Most of the time, the things that really change the world exist for something fundamentally selfish and then the world-changing ends up being a side-effect of that.

— ANDREW MASON

H ave you ever really had a good look, possibly with the aid of a magnifying glass, at the list of possible side effects for some medications? You might be trying to combat a cough but the long, long list of possible side effects folds out into an origami-like accordion of things you've never heard of, some potentially fatal, others you don't really want to know about, and usually you just fold it back up into a lotus flower and throw it away.

Common side effects of ESD include, but are not limited to, and these possible results are not a direct indication that past results equal future results ... OK, enough with my attempt at pharmaceutical legal humor.

Possible ESD Side Effects

1. a lofty, carefree attitude that might get you pulled over and asked for your ID and registration,
2. occasional bouts of silly pranks that would make your 8-year old proud,
3. just when you think you're going to give up, when you think it's just not worth it, something gives, kicks in, and you leapfrog to a point beyond what you expected,
4. bursts of pride to the point where tears come to your eyes at how far you've come,
5. accidental laughter at things others might not think are funny,
6. inside jokes that are so deep that no one gets them but you (and maybe me), but you laugh anyway,
7. changes occur in your life that you didn't expect, dream up, or even imagine. This usually occurs after repeated use,
8. a strong sensation that you want to go to sleep so you can get started on the morning and jump into another day,
9. dominoes fall into line unexpectedly, things happen in your life that you didn't expect,
10. bold thoughts that you can now do anything you put your mind to,
11. very rarely, but occurrences have been spotted in the wild of those who think they not only can do anything, but can do everything (they've been safely captured and brought back to the "I can do anything" level),
12. regular levels of boundless energy that you haven't felt for years--if ever,
13. slight flutters in your throat that usually come up from your gut and although you might want to clear your throat, the sensation then rises up further into the area of your brain just behind your eyes and there's a sense of

awe (if this happens, stay calm and let it roll through
you),

14. heart beats that you can feel in your bottom lip as it
trembles from the overwhelming love that you feel for
yourself,

15. and others.

As I look back at this list, I realize one might think, "Whoa. That's
crazy talk. That's a crazy person right there. Yes. Uh huh." And
"crazy" might not be that far off. But crazy is like "pretty" in my opinion: it's just that: an opinion, a perspective. For others it might seem
crazy, but for you or me, it might be admirable. It might even be
pretty. It might look good on you.

When you're just starting out (Passion), they might call you crazy.
At some point (Perseverance), they might take notice and call it cute
or even cool. When you're hovering above them as your feet barely
touch the ground, they call you by your first name and quiver in
respect (Play).

Whew. Can you see it?

Back to that list of side effects. There is one side effect that I won't
joke about.

I don't use the word "transformation" lightly. There's change,
which is more along the lines of "I no longer use the whitening toothpaste. I've changed. Now I use the sensitive gum toothpaste." Then
there's transformation.

A caterpillar turns into a butterfly. That's transformation. It was
this blob of squishy goo and it transformed into an unfathomable
array of colors and speckles that seems to have no place in this
natural world--except that it's exactly at home.

Your natural, true self is more at home in this world than the self
you were before.

There's a chance that you will transform from a person you used
to be to a person you now are. Now don't quiz me on DNA and blood
and cells and neurons, but I believe that we can change who we are.

Sure, our fingerprint is still the same. That retina scan when you walk into your CIA job will still register the same person as it did before, but something has changed, no, transformed, within you.

One side effect is that you might need to get used to your new self. That right there can take some adapting. But the more common side effect that can be challenging is when others don't quite know what to do with you.

Some might honest and truly prefer the Old You. They want the You of the past, the one before you morphed into the person you were meant to be.

Others might try to hide it, but still others might be openly jealous of where you've gone. They might try to sabotage your progress so you'll get back to the level where *they* exist. Then there's a decision to make.

If there are friends or family who just can't deal with this New You, you might have to decide whether or not you want them as prominently in your life. If Aunt Hilda only talks about how you used to be, back in the good old days, and has little to no respect for what you wanted, dreamed of, and have now achieved, it might be time to put Aunt Hilda into the I'll-see-you-at-the-next-family-reunion-Aunt-Hilda-drive-safe category.

It can be painful. Uncle Hobart, Aunt Hilda's darling but still stern husband, might take you aside and ask if you could just bring your Old Self back at least during the holidays so Aunt Hilda can rest in peace with her only niece or nephew. Yeah, that's a tough one. You could pretend to be the old you for a few hours and leave that self at the front door (or better yet, tossed down the toilet) when she leaves, but that Old Self doesn't exist in you anymore. It's just not who you are.

A related side effect is when Aunt Hilda (oh dear Aunt Hilda, she means so well!) shows genuine interest in your transformation, your change, your new life, and wants to know more about it, but you can't put it into words that she understands.

Here's a tip for that scenario. Don't try to bring Aunt Hilda along for the ride. Don't bother to try to get her to "understand" everything that you've been through. Keep it simple. Make it quick. Explain it as you might to the checker at the supermarket and know you have about three minutes to get it across and you'll never see her again. But with Aunt Hilda, at least look her directly in the eyes and put a hand on her hand so she knows you're serious, that you mean well, and that you care deeply about her. But that no, she doesn't need to completely understand that you have metaphysically transformed into another being, much like that caterpillar into a butterfly, but that you're happy now. That usually does the trick. "Aunt Hilda, I wasn't happy before with my life. Now I'm happy. Isn't that the most important thing? Now, would you like some more sour cream on your baked potato?"

Of course, Uncle Hobart is going to come at you with the logistics and realities of paying the mortgage and leading a good example for your kids. But you will pay the mortgage and what better role model for your kids could you be than to bring out the genuine, pure, unfiltered, raw, loving and full-of-energy awesome beast of an unstoppable, rocket-powered, fantastically talented creature that you are?

In fact, you can just say that to Uncle Hobart. He won't know what to do with it. But he'll usually stop asking about it. Make sure you emphasize "awesome beast." That will do the trick.

- Possible: side effects
- Impossible: don't deal with it
- Repossible: side benefits

Speaking of the mortgage ...

44

REALITY CHECK AND THE "OVERNIGHT SUCCESS"

A dream doesn't become reality through magic; it takes sweat, determination and hard work.

— Colin Powell

"Well, it's not magic."

You hear that often after people have put in hours or months or a lifetime of hard work to get where they are. The "10 Years + 1 Overnight = Overnight Success" stories. ESD is also no silver bullet, it's not a quick fix, and it's certainly not a get-rich-quick scheme.

"It's hard work."

There is work involved. How much and how hard it becomes is up to you. Back in the chapter on flow, I talked about how we can reach a higher level of consciousness where "better work takes less time," to put it in corporate, MBA, scientific speak. I can't prove it. I don't have formulas or videos to back it up, but I just know that I have reached a place where better work takes me less time. Sure, a big part of that is because I absolutely love what I'm doing.

"Gotta pay the mortgage."

I'm paying the mortgage. I'll pay off the mortgage. I don't usually like making predictions, but I'm going to pay off the mortgage faster than I ever would have believed. There, I said it. But the "reality check" is that, and this might be hard to believe, I also care less about money than I used to. It used to be a goal of my writing: Best seller! Make a million! Sure, those milestones would be fun, but they're more scenic rest stops along the way. How is this possible? Because most of the work I'm doing these days is effortless and in fact supplies me with energy. That's how I'm going to pay the mortgage ... although the mortgage banker will raise an eyebrow.

It's OK, I got this.

- Possible: reality
- Impossible: magic
- Repossible: magical reality

45

WHEN YOU HEAR ABOUT HOW A PERSON CHANGED HER LIFE, IT CHANGES YOUR LIFE.

When people send you a story that has changed their lives, they are sending you a story that is filled with grace. They're saying this changed my life. When you read it, it changed your life.

— CAROLINE MYSS

E ven if you say you don't believe it, it can't be true, or is exaggerated, it gets you thinking.

Part of me doesn't even care how people changed their lives or if how or what they did is applicable to the reader. All I really want is the tiniest of sparks to ignite what may be, could be, just might be the start of something.

We often forget that we are inspirational to others. Also because we often don't inspire ourselves. One comment I often get is that I'm very hard on myself. I set high standards and then I don't stop until I reach them. Until I get there, I'm hard on myself. Yeah, I suppose it's true. But even that has been an inspiration to others: just the fact that I won't give up.

Some people think it's annoying, but to others it's inspirational.

See what I mean?

We don't know which stories will inspire others. We don't know even which part of which story might inspire someone you might never think would be inspired by that part of the story. See how small the chance is? But there's a chance.

Here's some more math about probability. The chance of someone else hearing your story goes down to zero when you don't tell your story. We haven't had any math problems for at least a few chapters:

You + Silence = Silence

I'm looking for people to interview who subscribe to a philosophy of Every Single Day. It's how tiny change on a daily basis can lead to big change. That's it. It's crazy simple. But it's not necessarily easy.

I want your stories to be told. I don't care if you've done handstands every day for three years or kissed a stranger Every Single Day for a month, those stories have changed who you are and by telling your stories there's a chance they will help change someone else's life.

Your story of the change in your life will change the life of someone else. It's probably a law of physics. But I wouldn't know. I only know about probabilities and there's a chance that your story will help to change someone else's life. Are you ready to tell it? Tell it to me.

Here's how: [https://goo.gl/bhWnt2]

- Possible: have a story to tell
- Impossible: tell everyone your story
- Repossible: tell your story

46

FREEDOM

The secret to happiness is freedom ... and the secret to freedom is courage.

— THUCYDIDES

I was asked what I truly, really, no jokes, deep down, really, really, really wanted. The first word that came to mind was: freedom.

Freedom from the chains of the past.

Freedom from the ever-present dream (or was it a nightmare?) that has been eating away at your soul since you can remember.

Freedom from the nagging, harassing, gnawing reminder that Every Single Day you weren't being who you knew yourself to be.

Freedom from the evil eye of others who question your Dream.

Freedom from the decision-making process that you no longer have to endure Every Single Day of your life. There is no longer a decision, you are free.

Freedom from the walls that held you back. From the mountains, the tiniest of pebbles under your shopping cart wheel, the invisible barriers that used to be so powerful over you.

Freedom from the nightmare that your dream would never see the light of day.

Freedom from the ghost of yourself who haunted you and is now banished as long as you keep up your ESD shield.

Freedom from whatever it was that was pinning you down.

Freedom from the smallest and largest of barriers in your future, for you now have the tools to overcome all of them or know when it's time to pivot and change course.

Freedom to put down this book and feel the confidence in yourself that you got this, you know what to do, and how to begin.

Freedom from the solitude of the deep and dark cavern of your dream that you never or rarely shared, but is now open to the world and you know you are not alone, that you have a team of ESDers who share your passion and courage and are with you, behind you, in front of you, all around you, and you know that you are no longer alone.

Freedom to begin.

Freedom to fall repeatedly, get up, and keep going.

Freedom to fail again and again, but know that you're learning from each failure.

Freedom to experiment with options, to treat them as a game or a test, and to improve on each iteration and focus on the goal and less on the outcome.

Freedom to speak from the bottom of your heart.

Freedom to let loose the shivers in your throat to say what you want to tell the world.

Freedom to live to the fullest of your potential, to unlock what you have been holding back, to get to the point where you think you can't go any more and then you go more, further, stronger than you ever were, on a second wind, with the power beyond yourself, to push and be pulled, to soar, coast, and sail at speed and heights that you never before imagined were possible for you.

Freedom to take a stand, draw a line in the sand, and only take steps, no matter how small, in the shoes of who you truly are.

- Possible: secret
- Impossible: hidden
- Repossible: freed

I am now free to end this book and you are free to move about the cabin.

Please check for your belongings in the overhead bins as contents have, hopefully, shifted since take off.

PART VIII

POSTSCRIPT

47

WHERE TO GO FROM HERE

"**There's a spark within me that has been relit.** I know ESD is the kindling I need to get the fire crackling and roaring ... there are flames here that need to breathe and light the world."

— P.C.

If there's anything I want you to remember from this book, it's that you don't have to embark on this journey alone.

Join the Every Single Day Community at esd. repossible.com to, as P.C. put it above, relight your spark and get the fire crackling and roaring.

- **Possible:** turn the page
- **Impossible:** ignore your spark
- **Repossible:** join the ESD Community

"Get busy living, or get busy dying."

— STEPHEN KING (FROM HIS SHORT STORY, "THE SHAWSHANK REDEMPTION")

AFTERWORD

By failing to prepare, you are preparing to fail.

— BENJAMIN FRANKLIN

This is not over.

There is no finish, done, completed. It's an ongoing love affair.

There is no finish line--at least not one that I'm looking for. I'm it for the race, for the thrill, for the feeling of running and not realizing that I'm running.

This is preparation for the rest of our lives or at least this next chapter of our lives. I'm prepared for whatever comes my way and if I'm not, I have the resources to figure out the path and take that first step in that new direction.

I have tools. I got skills. I know who I am and where I'm going.

This is not your last day. This is your first day.

As I wind down the roller coaster of this book I know exactly what I'm most looking forward to. I'm looking forward to what you're going to do next.

I would truly love to hear about it. Head on over here and post a note about where you're heading: facebook.repossible.com.

Remember as John Muldoon said in the Foreword, "We're all rooting for you."

Let's make today the first day of your own Every Single Day.

- Possible: destination
- Impossible: detour
- Repossible: journey

ACKNOWLEDGMENTS

I can't say with certainty that this book would exist in your hands if it weren't for John Muldoon. The right place at the right time with the right, well, the right everything. It was the Perfect Storm. I'm grateful that you were there to be the lightning to my thunder, John.

I can write real good. But with editors, I write even gooder. Adwynna MacKenzie and Laurie King pulled (read: forced) stories out of me when I didn't want to, removed an alarming number of "just" and "like" the likes of which I just had no idea that they were there, and challenged me to rise up and above.

But it's more than grammar and word choice. They forced me to rephrase, explain, cut out, and ask "What are you really trying to say here? Who is your audience? Who have you now become so that you can go back to that point in time and remember what it was like then to connect with that person just starting down this path? Write in that voice." Dang. Ouch. Painful stuff. But it's Better Together. We're better together and I thank you.

I'd also like to acknowledge my family. Although maybe less in the "supportive" role ("Dad, are you done with your daily thing yet? Didn't you do that yesterday? Let's play basketball.") and more in the "tolerate" role. I hope they will believe in me after this book. But they allowed me to write Every Single Day since that November 1, 2012 and they, finally, just let me do my thing and knew when I was done I could play basketball. Thank you for being there and in one of the next books we can bring Li & Lu back to life and see how they've grown since the adventures in the "Markree Castle" series.

But it doesn't end there. I'm a firm believer in every little item along the way shapes who you are, where you're going, and how you're going to get there. Every nudge, pull, and yes, every wink provided a sparkle of light at the end of the road from everyone along the way. Thank you for allowing this to happen.

ABOUT THE AUTHOR

Bradley Charbonneau is an "unstoppable writing machine."

He can't not write. Writing gives him pleasure, perspective, and the chance to overuse the letter "p" whenever he feels like it.

He doesn't take himself terribly seriously—except for that daily writing habit he's got going on. He's truly reached Part 6: Play and isn't heading back down ever again.

All he really wants to do is tell stories, travel with his wife to oddball destinations by rickety transport, shoot baskets with his boys, try to perfect the burrito outside of California, and whisper the secrets of freedom and deep joy to whomever is within earshot and shares even the slightest inkling of curiosity.

He currently lives in a little town outside of Utrecht in The Netherlands with his wife Saskia, famous two young boys of "The Adventures of Li & Lu" fame, and their at-least-as-famous dog Pepper.

This is Bradley's sixth book.

It is far, far, far from his last.

Find, ask, discuss, play at:
bradleycharbonneau.com

[f] facebook.com/bradley.charbonneau.author
[twitter] twitter.com/brathocha
[instagram] instagram.com/brathocha

ALSO BY BRADLEY CHARBONNEAU

Most of my books are also available as audiobooks (which I giddily narrate). Search for my name at your favorite audiobook distributor, slip on your headphones, and let me take you away.

Repossible

1. Repossible
2. Every Single Day (+ Playbook)
3. Ask
4. Dare
5. Create
6. Decide
7. Meditate
8. Spark
9. Surrender
10. Play
11. Celebrate
12. Evaluate
13. Elevate
14. Share

Authorpreneur

1. You Don't Have to Write a Book (2021)
2. Write
3. Publish
4. Market
5. MailerLite for Authors
6. Audio for Authors

7. Meditation for Creatives (2021)

Frequency

1. Every Single Day
2. Every Single Day Playbook
3. Every Single Week
4. Every Single Month
5. Every Single Year
6. Every Single Life
7. *Every Single Day Teens (I want to write this one because I want to read this one...)*

Charlie Holiday

1. Now Is Your Chance
2. Second Chance
3. Chance of a Lifetime

Short Trips

1. Secret Bus to Paradise
2. Where I (Already) Am
3. Pass the Sour Cream
4. A Trip to Hel
5. Drive-By Dropping

Li & Lu

1. The Secret of Kite Hill
2. The Secret of Markree Castle

3. The Key to Markree Castle
4. The Gift of Markree Castle
5. Driehoek

Really Old ...

urban travel guide SAN FRANCISCO

EXCERPT FROM "ASK"

THE NEXT BOOK IN THE REPOSSIBLE SERIES

E very Single Day, the book you have in your hands, was the beginning of my tiny steps towards something big.

"Big" has arrived.

I didn't know when I wrote this book that it would blossom into the 14-book "Repossible Series" that it now is.

The next book in the series and, in a way, the first book in the Repossible Roadmap, is: *Ask.*

The subtitle is, "What if the answer is yes?"

Here's an excerpt from *Ask.*

Prologue

"The fact that you are willing to say, 'I do not understand, and it is fine,' is the greatest understanding you could exhibit."

— WAYNE DYER

SINCE I'VE GRADUATED from the *School of Not Asking* and am now in the part-time accreditation program of *Asking All the Time*, I need to revisit my days of fear.

It's a Friday afternoon as I write this. I just got a text from my 16-year-old son Liam that he didn't do very well on his German test.

His mother and I speak fluent German. I asked him yesterday (and over the past two years...) if I could help him with studying.

- I asked.
- I begged.
- I pleaded.

Then I forced it and just spoke German and kept at it.

But he wasn't having any of it. He wanted to do it his way. He didn't want our help. He said he was *fine*. He had a *good study session*.

Had he received a good grade, this would have all been fine. Had he any sort of grasp on German, I'd be OK with this.

But he didn't and he doesn't.

- He didn't ask for help.
- He even refused help.
- He's 16.
- He's a boy.

I sent him a text after his test saying something along the lines of how asking for help was not a sign of weakness but rather **those who are strong ask questions to become even stronger.**

Yes, not only do I put brilliant quotes in the beginnings of chapters of my books, I also send texts to my kids.

You are voluntarily reading this book. Well, unless you're in a prison in Thailand and this was the only English book left on the cart.

But for my kids, I like to think that they "hear me even if they're not listening."

Maybe they want the answers even though they don't dare ask.

I have long gotten over my fear of asking. I ask for anything—and everything—these days. No shame. No fear. No problem.

Sure, I get in trouble. But what I really want to do is **begin the conversation.**

That's what I'm doing here with you.

You see, I have no idea where you are along the spectrum of Ask.

1. You don't dare
2. You might but you don't really want the answer—or want to talk about it
3. You don't really want to know at all
4. You ask a bit—but maybe just the easy stuff
5. You ask the medium stuff
6. You can deal the hard stuff
7. You want the hard stuff and relish it
8. You're practically a mercenary "ask" professional who even asks for those who don't dare

But I want to start from the beginning. It's almost a birth or a seed sprouting from its little egg or shell or...whatever it is that a seed comes from.

See? I'm asking questions already. "Where does a seed come from? What does it break out of?"

I don't know. I'm asking.

I'm not afraid to ask the silly stuff.

You know why?

Because it's practice. Then I get more used to it and I can ask the harder stuff:

1. What is this next paragraph about?
2. What is this book about?
3. What is the Repossible series really uncovering?
4. Who am I to write it?

Wow. Dang.

Pipe down there, Pendergrass.

See how quickly things can get out of hand?

Let's stick to the easy stuff at first. For example:

"Should we turn the page and get started with asking?"

Ask is available at many fine stores: books2read.com/ask/.

THE END

Thank you for reading Bradley Charbonneau's "Every Single Day."

With, what, something like seven chapters after that last chapter, I just wanted to put this in here to say that it's over, it's done ... or rather, depending on what day it is and if this day happens to be the first day of the rest of your life, then welcome to the beginning.

Thank you, thank you, thank you for reading.

From Driebergen, The Netherlands, this has been Bradley Charbonneau.

Manufactured by Amazon.ca
Bolton, ON

17841555R00111